Biotic Inventory in the Schwoebel Tract at Valley Forge National Historical Park

Technical Report NPS/NER/NRTR—2006/068

Richard H. Yahner, Jacob E. Kubel[1], and Bradley D. Ross[2]

School of Forest Resources
The Pennsylvania State University
University Park, PA 16802

[1]current address
Natural Heritage & Endangered Species Program
Massachusetts Division of Fisheries and Wildlife
1 Rabbit Hill Road
Westborough, MA 01581

[2]current address
734 Partridge Lane
State College, PA 16803

November 2006

U.S. Department of the Interior
National Park Service
Northeast Region
Philadelphia, Pennsylvania

The Northeast Region of the National Park Service (NPS) comprises national parks and related areas in 13 New England and Mid-Atlantic states. The diversity of parks and their resources are reflected in their designations as national parks, seashores, historic sites, recreation areas, military parks, memorials, and rivers and trails. Biological, physical, and social science research results, natural resource inventory and monitoring data, scientific literature reviews, bibliographies, and proceedings of technical workshops and conferences related to these park units are disseminated through the NPS/NER Technical Report (NRTR) and Natural Resources Report (NRR) series. The reports are a continuation of series with previous acronyms of NPS/PHSO, NPS/MAR, NPS/BOS-RNR, and NPS/NERBOST. Individual parks may also disseminate information through their own report series.

Natural Resources Reports are the designated medium for information on technologies and resource management methods; "how to" resource management papers; proceedings of resource management workshops or conferences; and natural resource program descriptions and resource action plans.

Technical Reports are the designated medium for initially disseminating data and results of biological, physical, and social science research that addresses natural resource management issues; natural resource inventories and monitoring activities; scientific literature reviews; bibliographies; and peer-reviewed proceedings of technical workshops, conferences, or symposia.

Mention of trade names or commercial products does not constitute endorsement or recommendation for use by the National Park Service.

This report was accomplished under Cooperative Agreement 4000-8-9028, Supplemental Agreement Number 36 with assistance from the NPS. The statements, findings, conclusions, recommendations, and data in this report are solely those of the authors, and do not necessarily reflect the views of the U.S. Department of the Interior, National Park Service.

Reports in these series are produced in limited quantities and, as long as the supply lasts, may be obtained by sending a request to the address on the back cover. When original quantities are exhausted, copies may be requested from the NPS Technical Information Center (TIC), Denver Service Center, PO Box 25287, Denver, CO 80225-0287. A copy charge may be involved. To order from TIC, refer to document D-089.

This report may also be available as a downloadable portable document format file from the Internet at http://www.nps.gov/nero/science/.

Please cite this publication as:

Yahner, R. H., J. E. Kubel, and B. D. Ross. 2006. Biotic inventory in the Schwoebel tract at Valley Forge National Historical Park. Technical Report NPS/NER/NRTR—2006/068. National Park Service. Philadelphia, PA.

Table of Contents

Table of Contents (continued)

Figures

Tables

Appendixes

Appendixes (continued)

Summary

As national parks and other public lands become more insular from increased habitat fragmentation, these lands will be essential for maintaining floral and faunal diversity as well as the functional integrity of ecosystems throughout the eastern United States (Ambrose and Bratton 1990; Yahner 2000). Inventory data on flora and fauna provide an understanding of relative abundance and distribution of park biota and, therefore, aid in creation and evaluation of management plans for certain species. The National Park Service (NPS) has determined a need for comprehensive information about the biological resources on the Schwoebel tract (acquired in August 2004) to complement recently conducted inventories of amphibians and reptiles (hereafter termed herpetofauna; Tiebout 2003a; Yahner 2006a), mammals (Yahner et al. 2006a, 2006b), birds (Yahner et al. 2001a), and vegetation (Lundgren et al. 2002) at Valley Forge National Historical Park (VAFO). The objectives of our inventory were to document (1) presence, relative abundance, and distribution of herpetofauna, mammals, and birds on the Schwoebel tract, and (2) presence of woody plant species on the Schwoebel tract.

We surveyed herpetofauna, mammals, birds, and woody plants between 9 February–28 October 2004 using opportunistic observations (all taxa) and general search (herpetofauna), anuran-calling (herpetofauna), artificial cover-object transect (herpetofauna), live-trapping (mammal), spotlighting (mammal), point-count (birds), and owl (birds) surveys. We detected 11 species of herpetofauna, including four salamander, four anuran, one turtle, and two snake species on the Schwoebel tract at VAFO. All herpetofauna were species documented previously at VAFO (Tiebout 2003a), and none was recognized as a federal or state species of special concern. We documented 14 species of mammals on the tract with only one species of weasel (*Mustela* spp.) not documented previously at VAFO. None of the mammal species was recognized as species of special concern. Additionally, we observed 73 bird species during 2004 on the Schwoebel tract, including seven species listed federally as birds of conservation concern and/or Audubon WatchList species. Most notably, four of the species of concern (American woodcock [*Scolopax minor*], willow flycatcher [*Empidonax traillii*], wood thrush [*Hylocichla mustelina*], and Louisiana waterthrush [*Seiurus motacilla*]) potentially bred on the tract. All species were detected previously during a recent bird inventory at VAFO (Yahner et al. 2001a). While conducting surveys of vertebrates we documented 78 species of woody plants via opportunistic observations. Forty-eight woody plant species were considered new records for the tract, as they were not included in the vegetation alliances used to describe the Schwoebel tract during the most recent vegetation-mapping project conducted at VAFO (Lundgren et al. 2002).

In conjunction with recently completed herpetofauna, mammal, and bird inventory projects and vegetation mapping at VAFO, information acquired during our research project on the Schwoebel tract will be included with the extensive long-term database of flora and fauna at VAFO. Data obtained during our inventory contribute to an understanding of presence, relative abundance, and distribution of species within VAFO. Based on knowledge and information derived from inventories of flora and fauna, resource management specialists will be able to make informed decisions on how best to manage natural resources within the national parks.

Acknowledgments

The National Park Service provided funding for the amphibian, reptile, mammal, bird, and woody plant inventory project on the Schwoebel tract at Valley Forge National Historical Park (VAFO). We appreciate cooperation of National Park Service personnel, especially Mr. John Karish, Chief Scientist of the National Park Service Northeast Region, and Ms. Margaret Carfioli, Ecologist at VAFO. We extend our thanks to Mrs. Emily Hill, Staff Assistant V at The Pennsylvania State University for her clerical assistance.

Introduction

The National Park Service (NPS) has determined that park managers need comprehensive information about biological resources in parks in order to maintain biodiversity and natural ecosystems (NPS 2000). As large tracts of public lands, such as national parks, become more insular from increased habitat fragmentation due to urbanization and changing land uses, these lands increasingly will be valuable for long-term maintenance of faunal diversity and functional integrity of landscapes and ecosystems in the eastern United States (Ambrose and Bratton 1990; Yahner 2000). One of the first steps required to achieve the NPS goal of conserving biodiversity in national parks is to conduct baseline inventories of vertebrate and plant species in the parks. Data from such inventories provide an understanding of relative abundance and distribution of park biota and, therefore, aid in the development of resource management plans and actions.

Several biological research projects have been conducted recently at VAFO. These include protocol tests for surveying amphibians, reptiles (Lutcher 1996; Carfioli 1998, Yahner et al. 1999; Carfioli 2000; Tiebout 2003a), mammals (Yahner et al. 1997), and birds (Yahner et al. 2001a). Additionally, a vegetation-mapping project is near completion at the park (Lundgren et al. 2002).

Although those projects added considerable knowledge about biological resources at VAFO, park managers have expressed needs for additional data. VAFO acquired a parcel of land in August 2004 known as the Schwoebel tract (later renamed "Waggonseller Farm"), but few data about wildlife or plants on the tract are available. Natural resources on the Schwoebel tract were not inventoried by the NPS prior to February 2004, and, therefore, represented an information gap for VAFO. Although researchers conducting the vegetation-mapping project (Lundgren et al. 2002) characterized vegetation on the Schwoebel tract, a complete inventory of vascular plant species has not been conducted for the property.

Given the gaps in knowledge about presence, distribution, and relative abundance of terrestrial vertebrates and plants on the Schwoebel tract and within other areas of VAFO (e.g., Asbestos Release Site Areas of Concern), we conducted a three-part, 1-year-long inventory project during 2004, with the findings of each part published in a separate report. The first part (Yahner et al. 2006a) consisted of inventories of herpetofauna and small mammals in the Asbestos Release Site Areas of Concern (hereinafter referred to as the ARS inventory project). The second part (this report) consisted of inventories of herpetofauna, mammals, birds, and woody plants in the Schwoebel tract (hereinafter referred to as the Schwoebel inventory project). The third part (Yahner et al. 2006b) was a parkwide inventory of mammals at VAFO. For the Schwoebel inventory project, we inventoried herpetofauna, mammal, bird, and woody plant species in order to address the information gap and update the list of documented taxa at VAFO.

The objectives of the Schwoebel inventory project were to document presence, relative abundance, and distribution of herpetofauna, mammals, and birds on the Schwoebel tract, and presence of woody plant species on the Schwoebel tract.

Study Area

Valley Forge National Historical Park (VAFO) was established in 1976 to commemorate the 6-month encampment of George Washington's army at Valley Forge during the Revolutionary War. The park consists of 1,408 ha (3,479 ac) in Montgomery and Chester counties, southeastern Pennsylvania; approximately 1,316 ha (3,254 ac) were under federal ownership during this study. VAFO is surrounded by industrial, commercial, and residential development, as well as major highways to the north, south, and east. The topography is relatively gentle, with rolling uplands and low hills; elevation ranges from 18–161 m (59–528 ft) (Tiebout 2003a). Of the total acreage under federal ownership, 374 ha (924 ac) are forest (relatively mature woodlands and plantations), 362 ha (894 ac) are grassland (mowed not more than once per year), 181 ha (447 ac) are successional forest (old-fields and relatively young woodlots with open or patchy canopy), 135 ha (334 ac) are lawn, 120 ha (297 ac) are developed (buildings, roads, parking lots, etc.), 57 ha (141 ac) are wetland (small ponds, rivers, wet meadows, etc.), 45 ha (111 ac) are cropland, and 42 ha (104 ac) are ornamental grove and nursery (Lundgren et al. 2002; Figure 1). The Schuylkill River is the major drainage and traverses the park from west to east.

The 29-ha (72-ac) Schwoebel tract is recently acquired land located in the northeastern portion of the park and consists of four cover-type classifications of vegetation communities (Figures 1 and 2). Old nursery (abandoned tree and shrub nursery in an early successional stage) and developed land (e.g., buildings, parking lots, and transportation corridors) are the two dominant cover types, accounting for approximately 67% and 21% of the total Schwoebel area, respectively. Grassland (non-mowed grass and pipeline right-of-way) and successional forest (old-field or young woodlot with open canopy), each, represent approximately 6% of the total area. Water (Myers Run, a 303[d]-listed impaired waterway) and forest cover (mature woodlot with closed canopy) are present, but these represent less than 1% of the area.

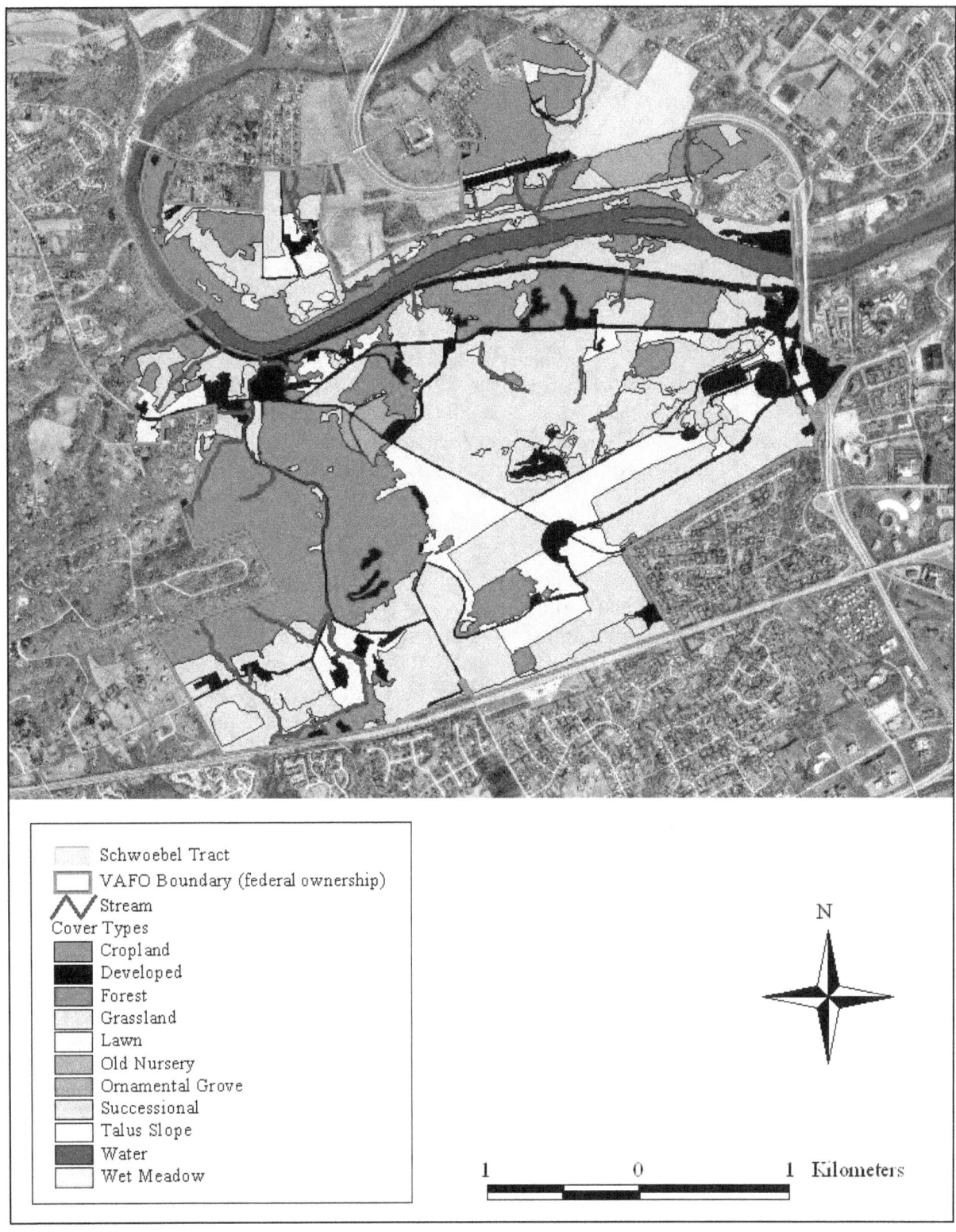

Legend:

- Schwoebel Tract
- VAFO Boundary (federal ownership)
- Stream

Cover Types
- Cropland
- Developed
- Forest
- Grassland
- Lawn
- Old Nursery
- Ornamental Grove
- Successional
- Talus Slope
- Water
- Wet Meadow

N

1   0   1   Kilometers

Figure 1. Location of the Schwoebel tract within Valley Forge National Historical Park (VAFO), Pennsylvania, and cover-type classifications of vegetation communities (Lundgren et al. 2002) for VAFO.

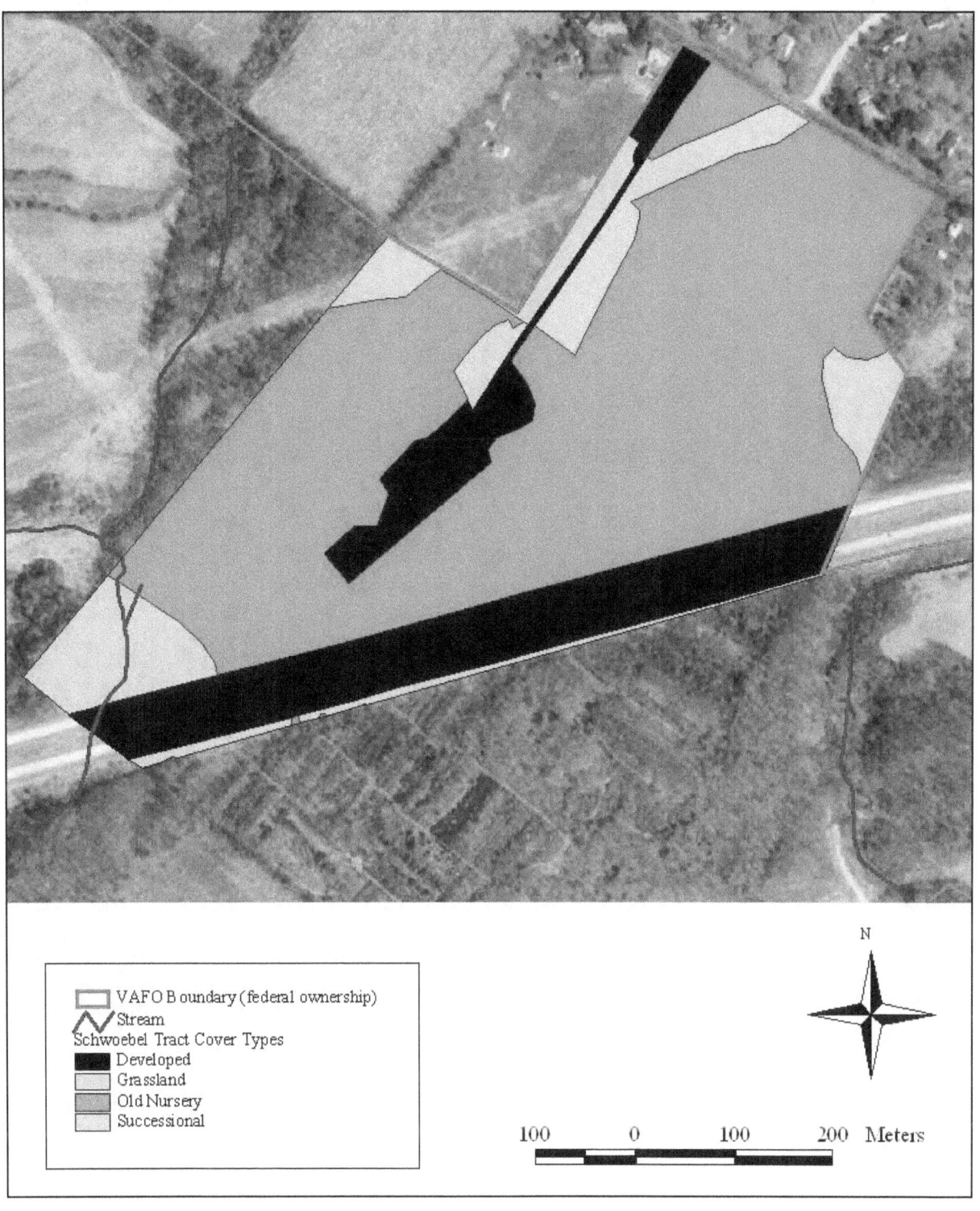

Figure 2. Cover-type classifications of vegetation communities (Lundgren et al. 2002) for the Schwoebel tract at Valley Forge National Historical Park (VAFO), Pennsylvania.

Methods

Documented and Predicted Species

As a first step, we reviewed published species range maps and the NPSpecies database of the National Park Service for information about known and potentially occurring species at VAFO and generated lists of species that could occur on the Schwoebel tract (Appendixes A–D). The NPSpecies database documents the occurrence of vertebrates and vascular plants in national parks based on information from a variety of reliable sources, such as published reports and museum records (NPS 2003). Information regarding birds, herpetofauna, fish, mammals, and plants at VAFO was updated in the NPSpecies database in March 2004. In addition, the database is updated periodically on an as-needed basis when new species are documented or inventory and research results are published (Jennifer Stingelin Keefer, NPSpecies Database Manager, The Pennsylvania State University, pers. comm., 2004). Herpetofauna and bird lists (Appendixes A and C) are based solely on records in the NPSpecies database because comprehensive inventories of these taxa have been conducted at VAFO (excluding the Schwoebel tract) within the past five years (Yahner et al. 2001a; Tiebout 2003a) and results of these inventories were catalogued in the database. However, a comprehensive inventory of mammals has not been conducted at VAFO, so our mammal list (Appendix B) is based on information from NPSpecies and published range maps (Burt and Grossenheider 1980; Merritt 1987). The current vegetation-mapping project (Lundgren et al. 2002) delineated vegetation alliances (Appendix E) within the Schwoebel tract and is the most reliable source of plant data. Therefore, our list of predicted woody plant species is based on species associated with vegetation alliances delineated in the vegetation-mapping project (Lundgren et al. 2002; Appendixes D and E).

Inventory of Herpetofauna, Mammals, and Birds

To meet objective 1 an in-depth inventory of herpetofauna, mammal, and bird species was conducted in the Schwoebel tract during 2004. Sampling effort was stratified among cover types for analysis of species richness, relative abundance, and distribution data; this allows natural resource management professionals at the park to address possible species- and habitat-specific management concerns. Sampling effort was allocated on the basis of the area of each cover type in proportion to the total area of the Schwoebel tract. Park personnel provided us with geographic information system (GIS) files that we used in combination with ArcView GIS 3.2 software (ESRI 2000) to develop a cover-type map of the Schwoebel tract. The GIS files, which are based on data collected during the vegetation-mapping project at VAFO (Lundgren et al. 2002), depict seven vegetation alliances within the Schwoebel tract; some alliances were classified in accordance with the National Vegetation Classification System (Grossman et al. 1998). We simplified the vegetation alliance information to create four cover types in order to locate survey transects and sampling points, (Figure 2; Appendix E). The four cover types represent practical classifications of vegetation communities based on the importance of vegetation structure in relation to general habitat requirements of various vertebrate species. The four cover types we used to classify vegetation communities were grassland, successional, old nursery, and developed. We defined grassland as non-mowed grassy areas lacking woody vegetation taller than grass; this cover type includes a pipeline right-of-way. We defined successional cover as pole stage or younger woodlots or old-fields/shrub lands with an open or patchy canopy, dense sub-canopy shrub layer, and substantial vine cover. We defined old nursery as habitat formerly used as a shrub and tree nursery. Old nursery represented an early successional forest community, but we made a distinction between old nursery and successional cover types because the dominant vegetation within old nursery cover consisted of ornamental and exotic species. We defined developed cover as areas dominated by an abiotic component (e.g., roads, parking lots, and buildings) and lacking native vegetation.

Herpetofauna

A majority of our sampling effort for inventorying herpetofauna focused on the old nursery cover type because it is the dominant cover type in the Schwoebel tract (Figure 2). However, a proportional amount of time was allocated to sampling other cover types and Myers Run, an intermittent stream located in the southwestern portion of the tract. Sampling protocols for herpetofauna consisted of techniques modified from monitoring protocols used to inventory VAFO (Tiebout 2003a, 2003b). These protocols included general searches, anuran-calling surveys, and artificial cover-object transects. Individuals were not marked in order to minimize handling of herpetofauna, and not all individuals could be captured and marked, so accurate capture/recapture information could not be obtained. Location, date, cover type, method, time elapsed, observer, and weather conditions were recorded for each herpetofauna survey. Weather conditions were recorded at the beginning and end of each survey and included a sky code, wind scale, and ambient air temperature (in shade) as described by Tiebout (2003b). In addition to animals identified during surveys, opportunistic observations (visual, aural, and handled for identification of certain species) of herpetofauna were documented.

General Searches: We sampled for herpetofauna in all cover types using general searches. General searching was defined as actively searching for animals (e.g., turning cover objects, such as rocks and logs, scanning ground and water surfaces) and has been effective in determining the presence of certain taxa (Yahner et al. 2001b; Kubel et al. 2002; Tiebout 2003a). Yahner et al. (2001b), Kubel et al. (2002), and Tiebout (2003a) reported that general searching accounted for all or nearly all species detected during inventories that used several other sampling techniques. For this reason, general searching was the primary method used to inventory herpetofauna in the Schwoebel tract.

General searches consisted of surface and substrate searches. Surface searches involved scanning the ground surface of terrestrial habitats, water surface of Myers Run, and vegetation overhanging the stream during daylight and nighttime hours. Additionally, we searched surfaces of buildings and other anthropogenic structures for species, such as black rat snake (*Elaphe obsoleta obsoleta*), which are known to inhabit abandoned buildings (Yahner et al. 2002). While conducting the searches, we expected to encounter foraging, migrating, and breeding amphibians during wet and/or dark conditions and basking reptiles during warm and sunny conditions. In addition, we expected to locate amphibian eggs within vernal pools present in the tract. Animals identified during surface searches were released at the point of capture immediately following identification when handling of individuals was necessary to differentiate between species. Species, general location (with respect to a permanent sampling point location), and cover type were recorded for each individual identified. Additionally, area searched (ha) was recorded for each surface search. Surface searches were conducted periodically (e.g., once to several times per month) between February and October 2004 during a variety of weather conditions in order to maximize the number of different species encountered.

Substrate searches were conducted during daylight hours and involved turning existing cover objects in terrestrial and aquatic habitats and scanning ground and water surfaces beneath and within close proximity to the turned objects. Cover objects included rocks (>15 cm [6 in] in diameter), logs (woody debris >7 cm [3 in] in diameter and >30 cm [12 in] long), leaf litter that retained moisture, and substrates (e.g., trash) meeting the size requirements specified for rocks and logs. Objects that were too large to turn or return to original positions after turning were not surveyed. In order to avoid potential disturbance of undiscovered artifacts, objects that were embedded (>5 cm [2 in]) in the soil were not turned. We expected to encounter salamanders and snakes during substrate searches. Individuals were captured, identified to species, and placed adjacent to the object after the object was returned to its original position. We recorded species, general location (with respect to a permanent sampling point location), cover type, and specific location (type of substrate) for each individual identified. Total area searched (ha) and number of objects turned were recorded by cover type for each search. Substrate searches were conducted approximately once per month between March and October 2004 and covered as much of the tract as possible.

Anuran-calling Surveys: Toad and frog species (Order Anura) can be distinguished by their vocalizations and typically are heard more often than seen (Shaffer 1991). Therefore, we used anuran-calling surveys to supplement general searching techniques (Yahner et al. 1999). Calling surveys involved standing in close proximity (10–20 m [33–66 ft]) to Myers Run and listening for calls of different frog and toad species. Only 125 m (410 ft) of stream flows through the southwest corner of the Schwoebel tract (Figure 2), so we established a single calling survey point midway along this portion of Myers Run (Figure 3). We visited the calling survey point for a 10-min period when calling activity is greatest (e.g., on wet or humid evenings between 30 min after sunset and midnight), and recorded the number of individuals of each anuran species heard during the survey. If individuals could not be distinguished, the minimum number of individuals that could be distinguished was recorded, and we noted that an additional, undetermined number of individuals were present. Individuals were classified as occurring inside or outside a 50-m (164-ft) radius of the survey point and within or beyond the boundary of the tract. We conducted calling surveys once or twice per month from March through July 2004 due to increased intensity of calling activity by different anuran species throughout spring and early summer months (Shaffer 1991).

Artificial Cover-object Transects: Artificial cover objects, such as flat boards and plastic sheeting, have been used successfully to document presence and relative abundance of several herpetofauna (DeGraaf and Yamasaki 1992; Fitch 1992; Kjoss and Litvaitis 2001; Kubel et al. 2002). We used artificial cover-object transects to supplement general searches and anuran calling surveys. Each transect traversed 100 m (328 ft) and contained 10 points established at 11-m (36-ft) intervals (Tiebout 2003a). Each point consisted of three flat boards (Tiebout 2003a) and a black plastic sheet (Kjoss and Litvaitis 2001; Kubel et al. 2002) spaced 0.5–1.0 m (1.6–3.3 ft) apart (Figure 4). The three boards included a small (30 x 30 x 2.5 cm [12 x 12 x 1.0 in]), undried white oak (*Quercus alba*) board, a medium (107 x 20 x 2.5 cm [42 x 8 x 1.0 in]), undried white oak board, and a large (122 x 61 x 1.25 cm [48 x 24 x 0.49 in]) plywood board (Droege et al. 1997; Tiebout 2003a). The black plastic sheet was 305 x 122 cm (120 x 48 in), and

9

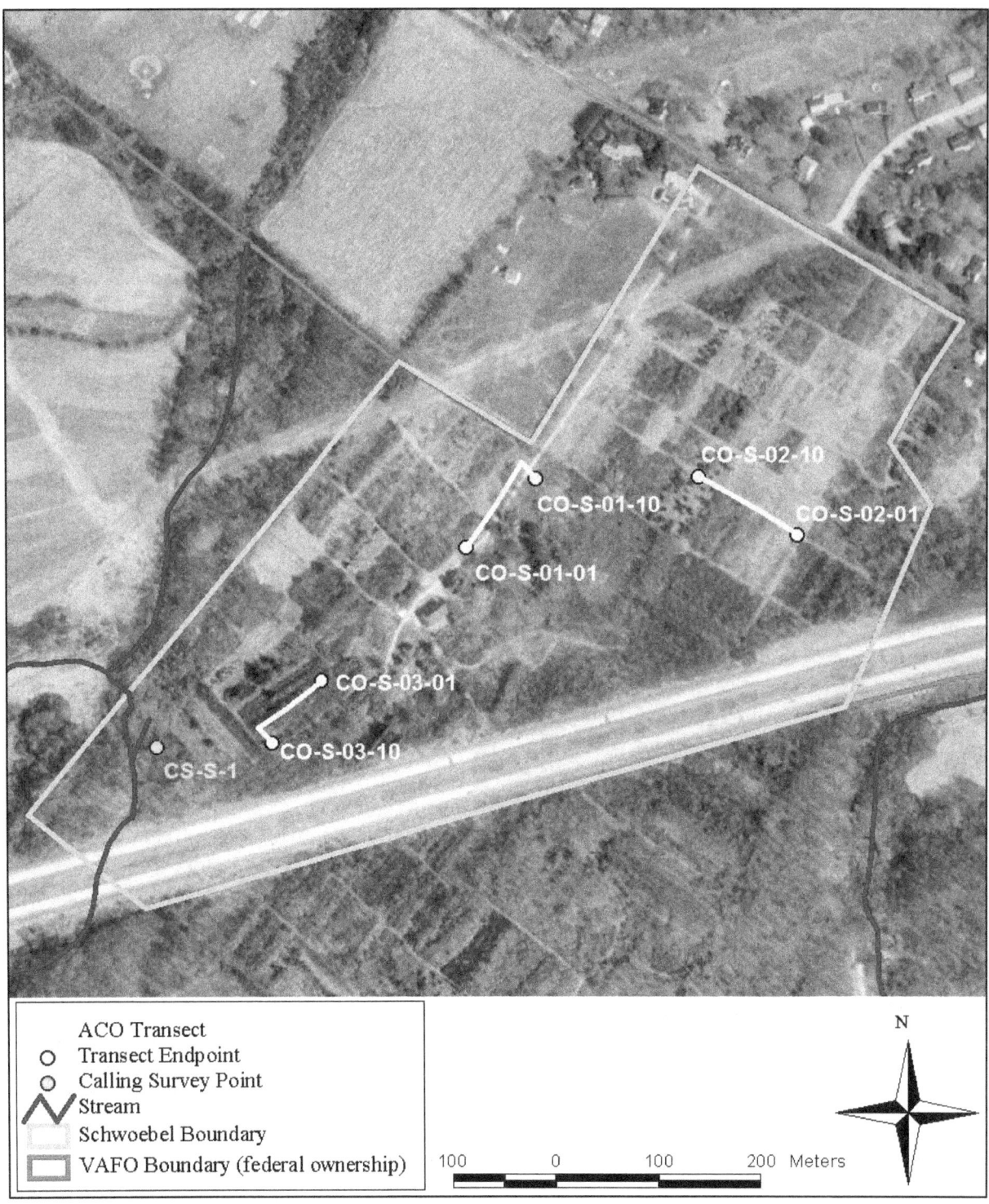

Figure 3. Sampling locations for artificial cover-object (ACO) transects and anura calling surveys conducted during 2004 on the Schwoebel tract at Valley Forge National Historical Park (VAFO), Pennsylvania.

sheet thickness was negligible. We expected to encounter salamanders under small and medium boards and snakes under medium and large boards and plastic sheets.

Boards and sheets were placed flat on the surface of the ground, with the exception of the large board, which was propped several centimeters at one end with a piece of wood to allow large-bodied herpetofauna to go beneath. Loose debris, such as leaf litter and stones, was cleared from under small and medium boards so that boards remained flush with the soil surface. Loose debris was not cleared from beneath large boards or plastic sheets. Plastic sheets were anchored temporarily at the corners with 10.2-cm (4.0-in) long nails.

Three artificial cover-object transects were used to sample herpetofauna on the Schwoebel tract. Two transects were located in old nursery cover type, and a third transect was located in grassland. No transect was located in the successional cover type because this type provided conditions similar to the old nursery type for herpetofauna, and cost and labor involved with this protocol limited us to three transects. No transect was located in a developed area because this cover type does not consist of a natural substrate upon which to place cover objects. Placement of transects was based on the need for each transect to traverse only one cover type and to centrally locate transects within designated cover types (Figure 3).

Artificial cover objects were placed in the field in February 2004 and were checked twice per month from March through October 2004, with a minimum of six days between checks. Cover objects were checked by turning the cover objects and scanning the surface of the ground adjacent to and underneath the turned object. When present, loose litter was prodded or separated to detect hidden individuals. Individuals were captured, identified to species, and returned next to the cover object. For many salamander species, foraging activity away from cover occurs predominantly at night (Petranka 1998), so we were more likely to encounter salamanders under cover objects during the day. Additionally, during cooler seasons, snakes were more likely to use black plastic sheets during morning or late afternoon hours for thermoregulation purposes (Kjoss and Litvaitis 2001). Therefore, we surveyed artificial cover-objects from between an hour after sunrise until 11:00 am.

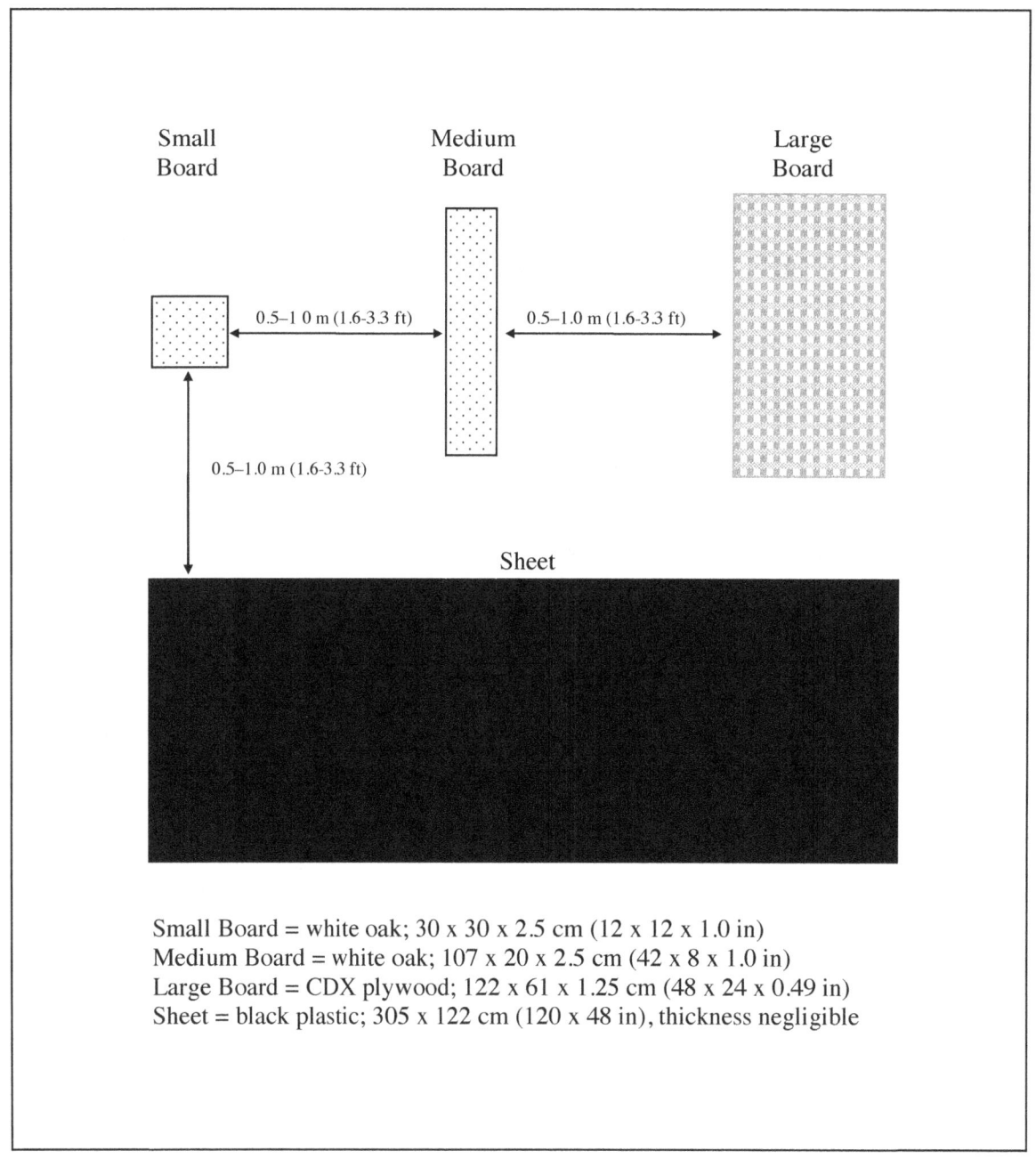

Figure 4. Schematic of a sampling point within a typical artificial cover-object transect used during the 2004 inventory of herpetofauna on the Schwoebel tract at Valley Forge National Historical Park, Pennsylvania. Each transect traversed 100 m (328 ft) and comprised 10 sampling points established at 11-m (36-ft) intervals (one point per interval).

Mammals

We conducted an inventory of mammalian species on the Schwoebel tract. At the Schwoebel tract mammals were categorized as either small (Norway rat [*Rattus norvegicus*] size or smaller) or large (larger than Norway rat in size), and separate sampling methods were used to inventory the two categories. Identification of bat species often requires an intensive sampling effort, specialized training, and direct handling of individuals, plus the NPS anticipated funding a survey for bat species during summer 2005, so we did not inventory bat species on the Schwoebel tract. Location, date, cover type, time elapsed, observer, and weather conditions were recorded for all mammal surveys. We recorded weather conditions prior to and following each survey, including a sky code, wind scale, and ambient air temperature (in shade) as described by Tiebout (2003b).

Small Mammals: Sampling effort for inventorying small mammals consisted of live-trapping (Yahner et al. 1997) grassland, successional, and old nursery cover types in the Schwoebel tract. We established sampling points for inventorying small mammals at 10-m (33-ft) intervals along transects. Transects were distributed evenly within undeveloped areas of the Schwoebel tract (Figure 5). We determined number, length, and location of transects to ensure that transects were located throughout the tract and that the number of sampling points per cover type was proportional to the total area of each cover type within the tract. Each sampling point consisted of a single Sherman live-trap (17.1 x 6.4 x 5.1 cm [6.7 x 2.5 x 2.0 in]). In order to avoid disturbance or destruction of traps, a limited number of sampling points were located in developed areas to target house mouse (*Mus musculus*) and Norway rat. Pitfall traps and drift fences were not used in this study because capture success does not tend to be greater with pitfall traps compared to live-traps (RHY, pers. obs.).

Sampling effort was based on 115 trap nights (approximately five trap nights per hectare of undeveloped habitat) between July–August and September–October 2004, giving a total of 230 trap nights in the Schwoebel tract. We defined a trap night as one trap set per night. Sampling effort consisted of nine trap nights each in grassland and successional cover and 97 trap nights in old nursery cover per season. We sampled all points in one night to avoid marking captured animals and assure each individual was a new capture for a given time period. Traps were baited with a small amount of peanut butter, placed flush with the ground surface, left open overnight, checked, and removed the following morning. Trap placement and checking did not require disturbance of the soil surface. We covered traps with herbaceous vegetation, leaf litter, or other debris to shade and insulate traps. We equipped traps with cotton to provide bedding for captured animals. Captured animals were identified to species and released. Dead animals were identified and left in the field for scavengers.

Large Mammals: Our objective for inventorying large mammals in the Schwoebel tract was to supplement the parkwide mammal inventory project (Yahner et al. 2006b) and list of documented mammal species at VAFO. Sampling strategies for large mammals included spotlighting surveys to identify species that tend to be crepuscular or nocturnal (rabbits, raccoon, fox, etc. [scientific names are provided in Appendix B]), opportunistic observations of animals or animal signs (e.g., tracks, scats, etc.), and live-trapping (Yahner et al. 1997). Spotlighting surveys were conducted between sunset and three hours following sunset. Surveys were conducted periodically (once to several times per month) March–October 2004.

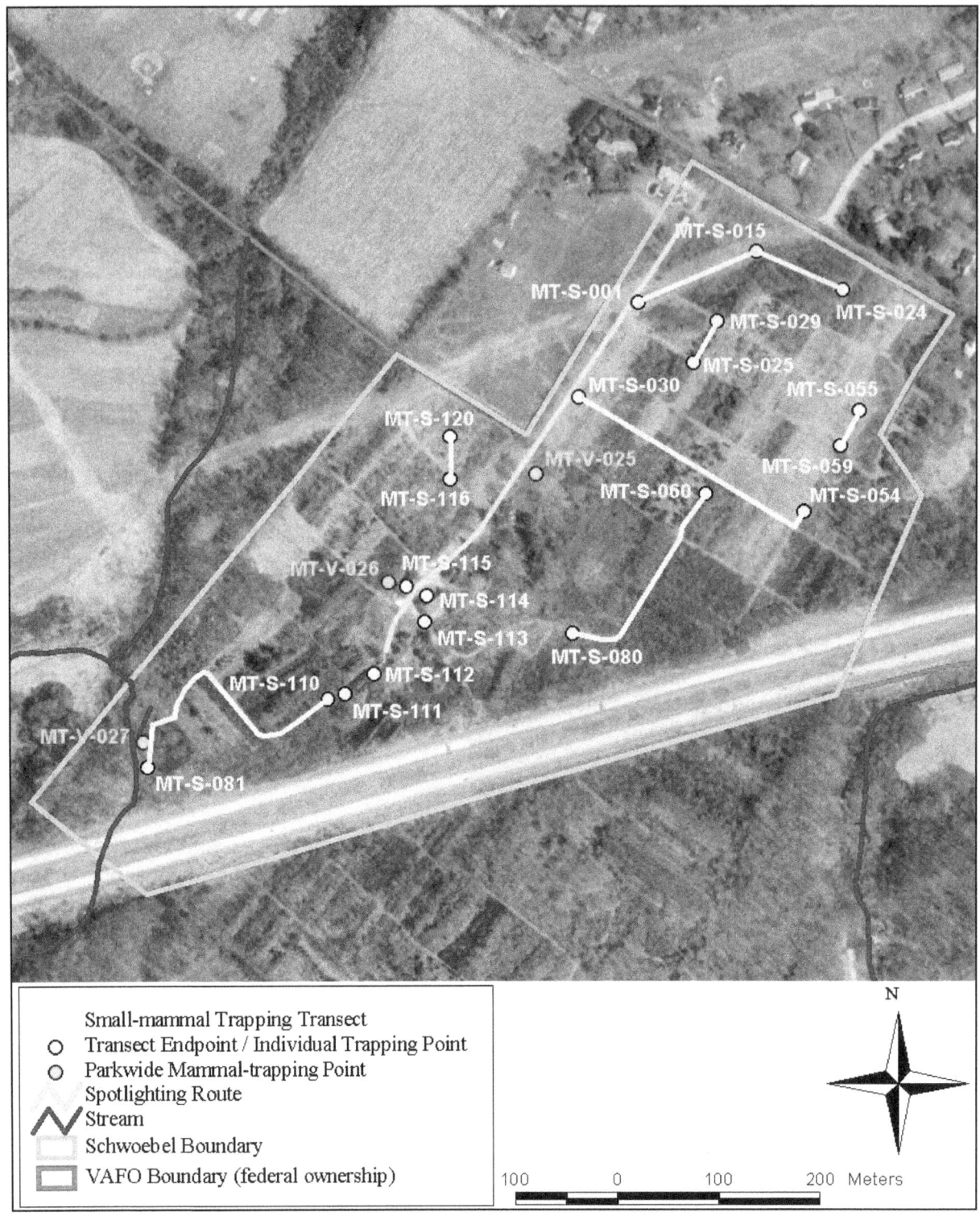

Figure 5. Sampling locations for small-mammal trapping conducted during 2004 on the Schwoebel tract at Valley Forge National Historical Park (VAFO), Pennsylvania, and for mammal trapping and spotlighting conducted in conjunction with the parkwide mammal inventory project (Yahner et al. 2005b).

Surveys consisted of slowly driving along the roadway that bisects the Schwoebel tract (0.3 km) and using vehicle headlights and a large flashlight to view animals in or near the driveway during nighttime hours (Figure 5). We recorded all species identified and distance (km) traveled for each survey.

Opportunistic observations consisted of visual identification of animals or animal signs that occurred at any time other than during a planned survey or identification of non-target animals during a planned survey (e.g., mammals detected under artificial-cover objects for herpetofauna). Opportunistic observations were recorded if the species had not been documented during the inventory project, the species was uncommon or rare at VAFO, the observed individual was abnormal (e.g., deformed, marked, etc.), or the observation included a large group of individuals (arbitrarily, >10 individuals). Not all mammals (i.e., weasels, voles) can be identified to the species level unless they can be examined closely or handled. For such opportunistic observations, individuals were identified to the genus level of taxonomic classification.

Live-trapping was used in conjunction with the parkwide mammal inventory project (Yahner et al. 2006b) in an effort to document species that had not been encountered during other inventory projects (Yahner et al. 2006a, 2006b) or while conducting other survey protocols. Species that we attempted to trap were termed "target species" and consisted of both small and large mammals including eastern fox squirrel, feral cat, house mouse, mink, smoky shrew, southern bog lemming, southern flying squirrel, and weasels (ermine and long-tailed weasel). Specifically, three points (MT-V-025, MT-V-026, and MT-V-027; Figure 3) were established for sampling weasels because of a sighting of an unidentified weasel there by J. Kubel during August 2004. Trapping occurred May–October 2004, with the majority of the trapping effort occurring July–October after most species were documented using other survey methods. We trapped at arbitrarily chosen locations in areas where undocumented species were expected to occur (e.g., based on habitat requirements) (Figure 5). At each point, we placed either a medium (13 x 13 x 41 cm [5 x 5 x 16 in]) or large (26 x 32 x 81 cm [10 x 13 x 32 in]) Tomahawk live-trap baited with meat or peanut butter to capture the target species. Number and type of traps, number of trapping periods, and length (days) of trapping periods at each sampling point were chosen arbitrarily because effectiveness of trapping efforts was difficult to determine. For instance, several factors can influence trapping success: 1) general degree of difficulty in live-trapping a particular target species, 2) likelihood that a target species occurs at or near a sampling point, 3) disturbance of traps by non-target species, and 4) weather conditions. The third factor was particularly problematic during this inventory, as baits placed in medium Tomahawk traps set for southern flying squirrels, weasels, or eastern fox squirrels often were stolen by mammals presumably too small to trigger the trap (e.g., white-footed mice). Conversely, Sherman traps and medium Tomahawk traps were triggered by mammals that attempted to take the baits but presumably were too large to enter the traps (e.g., common raccoons). To remedy these problems, we placed all types of traps at some sampling points in an attempt to capture common raccoons and white-footed mice and, hence, prevent them from disturbing traps set for other species. Traps were checked daily, and captures were identified to species and released. Dead animals were left in the field for scavengers.

<u>Birds</u>

Inventory protocols for birds on the Schwoebel tract included point-count surveys, owl surveys, and opportunistic observations (Yahner et al. 2001a). Point-count sampling points were distributed throughout the tract using a stratified random design. We placed sampling points using the following criteria, in order of importance: 1) approximately one point per 4 ha ($n = 7$ total points); 2) each cover type contained at least one point; 3) the number of points per cover type was proportional to the total area of each cover type within the tract; 4) points were ≥200 m (656 ft) apart; 5) points were ≥50 m (164 ft) from U.S. Rt. 422; and 6) when possible, points were located centrally within each cover type (arbitrarily, ≥25 m [82 ft] from a neighboring cover type). We used ArcView GIS 3.2 software (ESRI 2000) to generate randomly potential sampling points ($n = 350$) within the Schwoebel tract. Based on these criteria, we selected seven sampling points for point-count surveys on the Schwoebel tract (Figure 6).

Two surveys were conducted during four seasons: spring-migratory (15 April–25 May), breeding (25 May–15 July), fall-migratory (25 August–10 October), and winter (1 December–15 March) (Yahner et al. 2001a). Surveys occurred shortly after sunrise during spring-migratory and breeding seasons and between sunrise and 11:00 a.m. during fall-migratory and winter seasons. We conducted surveys on days with little or no precipitation and wind speeds less than 25 km/h (16 mi/hr). Location, date, cover type, starting time, and observer were recorded at each sampling point during a point-count survey. We recorded weather conditions at the beginning and end of each survey, including a sky code, wind scale, and ambient air temperature (in shade) as described by Tiebout (2003b).

Point-count surveys consisted of a 1-min equilibrium period followed by 10-min survey period (IBCC 1977; Fuller and Langslow 1984; Hutto et al. 1986; Verner and Ritter 1986; Buskirk and McDonald 1995; Dawson et al. 1995; Savard and Hooper 1995). We recorded all birds detected by sight or sound within and outside a 50-m (164-ft) radius. Observations of birds were recorded for the first three minutes, the first five minutes, and the total 10 minutes so they could be compared to data from studies that use these different lengths of time (Yahner et al. 2001a). No formal detection probability estimation analyses were conducted when presenting relative abundance of bird species. However, detectability of different bird species was considered when designing the inventory and analyses. We conducted bird point-count surveys during all seasons and different times of the day to maximize the probability of identifying all bird species (e.g., early morning during the breeding season to detect vocalizing males, and more than one hour after sunrise in the winter when foraging flocks become more active). Additionally, we conducted surveys only during periods of good weather (no precipitation and low wind) and for an extended time period (10 min) in order to maximize the probability of detecting all species and individuals at a sampling point.

Owl surveys were conducted during winter, 1 February–15 March 2004, at the Schwoebel tract using the nocturnal-owl survey protocol (Foster 1965; Lynch and Smith 1984; Morrell 1993). To avoid double-counting individuals, we established one nocturnal-owl survey point (OS-S-1) located adjacent to conifers (important cover and nesting habitat) and accessible during evening hours (Figure 6). To complement the inventory of five owl species conducted at survey point

Figure 6. Locations of sampling points for avian point-count surveys and owl surveys conducted during 2004 on the Schwoebel tract at Valley Forge National Historical Park (VAFO), Pennsylvania.

OS-S-1, we surveyed for barn owl (*Tyto alba*) adjacent to the old barn located within developed habitat on the tract (OS-S-2; Figure 6). We conducted two owl surveys from 1 February–15 March 2004 with the two surveys spaced at least two weeks apart. Surveys were conducted between one hour after sunset and one hour before sunrise on nights with little or no precipitation, winds <25 km/h (16 mi/h), and cloud cover less than 50%. Prior to each survey, we recorded date, starting and ending times, temperature (C), wind velocity (km/h), percent cloud cover (%), precipitation, and depth (cm) of snow cover.

At the survey point OS-S-1 we played calls of five owl species in the following order: saw-whet (*Aegolius acadicus*), eastern-screech (*Otus asio*), barred (*Strix varia*), long-eared (*Asio otus*), and great horned (*Bubo virginianus*) owl. Calls were played in this order to prevent limiting the response of small owls (potential prey to larger owls) by first broadcasting calls of larger predators (long-eared and great horned owl). Following a 1-minute equilibrium period, we played a call of saw-whet owl for 15 seconds. After 45 seconds of silence, we repeated two additional calling periods (call + 45 seconds of silence = calling period) and a fourth call by saw-whet owl followed by a 105-second silent period. We repeated this sequence (minus the equilibrium period) consecutively for each owl species at the survey point. At the survey point adjacent to the barn (OS-S-2), we played calls of barn owl following the protocol for saw-whet owl mentioned above. We recorded number and species of owls identified during the equilibrium, calling, and silent periods.

Opportunistic observations of birds were recorded during the inventory (9 February–28 October 2004) whenever we observed a species not yet documented on the Schwoebel tract. We recorded location, date, cover type, time, observer, and weather conditions for each observation.

Inventory of Woody Plants

In order to meet objective 2, we supplemented the existing list of woody plant species generated by the vegetation-mapping project at VAFO (Lundgren et al. 2002; Appendix E) by recording woody-plant species detected via opportunistic observations made while conducting vertebrate surveys on the Schwoebel tract at VAFO (Figure 2). We did not collect abundance information for vegetation on the tract, but this information is available in the vegetation-mapping report (Lundgren et al. 2002). We recorded location, date, and cover type for the first observation of every woody plant species identified.

Voucher Photographs

We did not collect voucher specimens of any taxon. Instead, we took photographs of species inventoried on the Schwoebel tract. JPEG files were created from the photographs and are on file with Mr. John Karish, Chief Scientist of the NPS Northeast Region, Ms. Margaret Carfioli, Ecologist at VAFO, and Dr. Richard H. Yahner, Professor of Wildlife Conservation, The Pennsylvania State University.

Global Positioning System Locations

We used a Trimble Pro-XR global positioning system (GPS) unit to identify locations of survey transects and sampling points. The GPS locations (Universal Transverse Mercator, Zone 18N) were stored electronically as ArcView shape files and used in combination with files provided by park personnel to create GIS data layers containing the post-processed survey locations. All GIS data layers were created using ArcView GIS version 3.2 software (ESRI 2000). Electronic copies of spatial data and associated Federal Geographic Data Committee compliant metadata will be provided following completion of the final report.

Information Storage

Relative abundance and species richness of herpetofauna, mammals, and birds, species richness of woody plants, and location of transects and sampling points on the Schwoebel tract are stored in hard copy and electronic format. Inventory data and locations are available in this report and in Microsoft Access computer files. ArcView shape files containing locations of the transects and sampling points and their accompanying UTM coordinates are available at Penn State and at the natural resource office in VAFO. Copies of this report, Microsoft Access computer files, and ArcView shape files are on file with Mr. John Karish, Chief Scientist of the NPS Northeast Region, Ms. Margaret Carfioli, Ecologist at VAFO, and Dr. Richard H. Yahner, Professor of Wildlife Conservation, Penn State. In addition to reports and GIS data layers, we provided information that will be used to update the records for VAFO in the Park Species section of the NPSpecies database. Relevant information from the inventory project was transferred into Microsoft Access format to satisfy requirements for the Vouchers and Observations section of the NPSpecies database.

Data Analyses

Data were compiled and summarized separately for herpetofauna, small mammals, and birds, with respect to species richness, relative abundance, and distribution on the Schwoebel tract. Species richness was compiled and summarized for woody plant species.

Herpetofauna

Species richness of herpetofauna was calculated as the total number of different species of herpetofauna inventoried using general searches, anuran-calling surveys, artificial cover-object transects, and opportunistic observations. Relative abundance of herpetofauna was calculated as the total number of individual herpetofauna by species detected during general searches, anuran-calling surveys, artificial cover-object transects, and opportunistic observations combined. All survey types were used in calculations of relative abundance of herpetofauna, but results were reported by survey type or a combination of certain survey methods when applicable. For example, relative abundance of salamander species was presented using a combination of results for general searches and artificial cover-object transects because salamanders are not vocal and were not targeted using calling surveys. Besides presenting species richness and relative abundance of herpetofauna, data on species richness and relative abundance were calculated and presented separately for amphibians (further divided into salamanders and anurans) and reptiles (further divided into turtles, snakes, and lizards). Information on distribution and precise location of individual herpetofauna within the Schwoebel tract is available in the Microsoft Access database that accompanies our final report.

Mammals

Species richness of mammals was calculated as the total number of different species of mammals inventoried using opportunistic observations, live-trapping, and spotlighting surveys. Relative abundances of small- and large-sized mammals were calculated as the total number of individual mammals detected by species during incidental observations and live-trapping (including the three parkwide live-trapping points located on the tract) and spotlighting surveys combined. All survey types were used in calculations of relative abundances of mammals, but results were reported by survey type when applicable. For instance, relative abundances of mammals were presented separately for live-trapping and spotlighting surveys because spotlighting surveys were designed to detect large-sized mammal species not targeted by live-trapping. Distribution and precise location of individual mammals on the Schwoebel tract are available in the Microsoft Access database that accompanies our final report.

Birds

Data obtained from surveying birds on the Schwoebel tract at VAFO were summarized to provide information about species richness and relative abundance of birds by season, survey method, and residency status, with emphasis on bird species of special concern (i.e., state and federally listed and Audubon WatchList). Species richness of birds was calculated as the total number of different species of birds inventoried using opportunistic observations, point-count, and owl surveys. Relative abundance was defined as the number of individual birds by species averaged over surveys (n = 2) and point-count sampling points (n = 7) on the tract. Relative abundance was calculated separately for each of the four seasons using results of point-count surveys. In conjunction with relative abundance, we presented the variability (standard deviation) among sampling points for the average number of individual birds by species over surveys. We presented relative abundance of bird species on the tract by season for long- and short-distance migrants and permanent residents. Long-distance migrants are bird species that reside outside of the continental United States and Canada during part of the year. Short-distance migrants are birds that migrate to other parts of the continental United States and Canada during part of the year. Permanent residents are defined as bird species present at VAFO throughout the year. Information on distribution and location of individual birds on the Schwoebel tract is available in the Microsoft Access database that accompanies our final report.

Woody Plants

Species richness of woody plants was calculated as the total number of different species of woody plants recorded. Information on location of individual plant specimens within the tract is available in the Microsoft Access database that accompanies our final report.

Results

We detected 98 animal species on the Schwoebel tract at VAFO from 9 February–28 October 2004 using opportunistic observations and general search, anuran-calling, artificial cover-object transect, live-trapping, spotlighting, point-count, and owl surveys (Table 1). Additionally, we recorded 78 species of woody plants while conducting surveys for vertebrates on the tract during 2004.

Herpetofauna

We detected four salamander, four anuran, one turtle, and two snake species on the Schwoebel tract at VAFO during 2004 using a combination of 17.5 hours of general searches (1,770 rocks and 112 logs surveyed), six anuran-calling surveys, 16 artificial cover-object transect surveys, and opportunistic observations (Appendix A). No egg masses or larvae were detected in vernal pools. All herpetofauna detected on the Schwoebel tract were documented previously during the most recent inventory of herpetofauna at VAFO (Tiebout 2003a). None of the 11 species of herpetofauna that we inventoried was federally endangered or threatened (USFWS 2005), or state endangered, threatened, critically imperiled, imperiled, or vulnerable (PANHP 2006).

All four salamander species (Appendix F) inventoried during the project were detected during general search surveys; whereas, redback and longtail salamanders (scientific names are given in Appendix A) were detected using artificial cover-object surveys. Northern two-lined salamander ($n = 63$ individuals) was the most abundant aquatic salamander, and redback salamander ($n = 36$, 19 lead-phase and 17 red-phase) was the most abundant terrestrial salamander, combining results from general searches and artificial cover-object transects.

All four anuran species (Appendix F) inventoried during the project were detected during general searches and by opportunistic observations. Northern spring peeper ($n = 40$ individuals) was the most abundant anuran species and was detected during all but artificial cover object transect surveys. Pickerel frog ($n = 24$) was the second most abundant anuran species on the Schwoebel tract and was detected during general search surveys and by opportunistic observation.

Eastern garter snake and northern black racer were the only snake species detected during the project (Appendix F). Artificial cover-object transects were the most effective method for locating snakes, with all 10 individuals detected using this protocol. One eastern box turtle was documented during a general search survey.

Mammals

We detected 14 mammal species on the Schwoebel tract at VAFO during 2004 using two live-trapping surveys for small mammals, five live-trapping surveys for large mammals, three spotlighting surveys, and opportunistic observations of animals and animal signs (Appendix B). Several species ranging in size from masked shrew to white-tailed deer were present on the tract. Thirteen species were documented previously at VAFO, and one weasel (ermine or long-tailed)

Table 1. Number of species by taxonomic group detected from 9 February–28 October 2004 on the Schwoebel tract at Valley Forge National Historical Park, Pennsylvania.

Taxonomic Group	Number of Species
Amphibians:	8
Salamanders	4
Anurans (frogs and toads)	4
Reptiles:	3
Snakes	2
Turtles	1
Lizards	0
Mammals	14
Birds	73
Woody plants	78

was predicted to occur within the park and was not recorded previously at VAFO (NPS 2004). We made an opportunistic observation of a weasel species, but unless trapped and examined closely for identifying characteristics, ermine and long-tailed weasel cannot be differentiated. None of the mammal species that we inventoried was federally endangered or threatened (USFWS 2005), or state endangered, threatened, critically imperiled, imperiled, or vulnerable (PANHP 2006).

We recorded the highest number of species ($n = 14$) using incidental observations. However, live trapping was required to classify some individuals (e.g., meadow vole) to the species level. We documented four mammal species (Virginia opossum, white-footed mouse, meadow vole, and common raccoon) using live-trapping surveys, with white-footed mouse and meadow vole being the most abundant species (59 and seven of 68 individuals captured, respectively; Appendix G). Two species of mammals were documented during spotlighting surveys, including white-tailed deer ($n = 4$) and red fox ($n = 1$).

Birds

We detected 73 bird species on the Schwoebel tract at VAFO from 9 February–28 October 2004 using eight point-count surveys (two per season), two owl surveys, and opportunistic observations (Appendix C). All species detected on the tract were detected previously during the most recent bird inventory at VAFO (Yahner et al. 2001a). Seven species of special concern used the tract at different times of the year (Table 2). Most notably, four species of special concern potentially bred on the Schwoebel tract, including American woodcock, willow flycatcher, wood thrush, and Louisiana waterthrush (scientific names are given in Appendix C).

Table 2. Bird species of special concern detected during spring-migratory, breeding, fall-migratory, and winter seasons, 9 February–28 October 2004 on the Schwoebel tract at Valley Forge National Historical Park, Pennsylvania.

Species	Status[a]	Season[b]
American woodcock	AW	winter and between winter and spring-migratory
black-billed cuckoo	BCC	spring-migratory
willow flycatcher	AW	spring-migratory and breeding
wood thrush	BCC & AW	spring-migratory and breeding
blue-winged warbler	AW	spring-migratory
prairie warbler	BCC & AW	spring-migratory
Louisiana waterthrush	BCC	spring-migratory

[a]Status of birds of special concern was determined from the following sources: federally endangered, threatened (http://www.fws.gov/endangered/wildlife.html) bird of conservation concern (BCC) (http://migratorybirds.fws.gov/reports/bcc2002); state endangered, threatened, critically imperiled, imperiled, or vulnerable (http://www.naturalheritage.state.pa.us/vertebrates.aspx); Audubon WatchList (AW) (http://www.audubon.org/bird/watch).
[b]Seasons: spring migration (15 April–25 May), breeding (25 May–15 July), fall migration (25 August–10 October), and winter (1 December–15 March).

Spring Migration

We found the highest number of bird species on the Schwoebel tract at VAFO during the 2004 spring-migratory season (n = 41, Appendix H). Five of the 10 most abundant bird species detected by point-count surveys were permanent residents, three species were short-distance migrants, and two were long-distance migrants (Appendix I). The four most common species were gray catbird (1.79 average number/point/survey), northern cardinal (1.71), American robin (1.36), and wood thrush (1.29).

Breeding Season

We observed 27 bird species while conducting point-count surveys on the Schwoebel tract at VAFO during the 2004 breeding season (Appendix J). Four of the 10 most abundant species observed were permanent residents, three species were short-distance migrants, and three were long-distance migrants (Appendix K). The four most common species were gray catbird (2.29 average number/point/survey), northern cardinal (2.00), wood thrush (1.79), and common yellowthroat (1.50).

Fall Migration

We observed 29 bird species while conducting point-count surveys on the Schwoebel tract at VAFO during the 2004 fall-migratory season (Appendix L). Unlike spring-migration and breeding seasons, nine of the 10 most frequently detected species were permanent residents, one species was a short-distance migrant, and none was a long-distance migrant (Appendix M). The four most common species were American robin (7.93 average number/point/survey), gray catbird (1.43), house finch (1.14), and Carolina chickadee (1.07).

<u>Winter Season</u>

We observed 29 bird species while conducting point-count surveys on the Schwoebel tract at VAFO during the 2003–04 winter season (Appendix N). Similar to fall-migratory season, the most abundant species tended to be permanent residents (Appendix O). Six species (golden-crowned kinglet, ruby-crowned kinglet, white-throated sparrow, dark-eyed junco, red-winged blackbird, and purple finch) were short-distance migrants, and the remaining 23 were permanent residents. The four most common species were Canada goose (2.93 average number/point/survey), red-winged blackbird (2.50), Carolina chickadee (1.64), and American robin (1.21).

Woody Plants

We identified 78 species of woody plants through opportunistic observations while conducting vertebrate surveys on the Schwoebel tract at VAFO (Appendix D). Twenty-five species that we documented were recorded previously, and six others were predicted to occur (not commonly encountered in the vegetation alliances during the vegetation-mapping project, but common to the alliances on a global scale) on the tract based on the vegetation alliances used to classify the Schwoebel property during the vegetation-mapping project at VAFO (Lundgren et al. 2002; Appendix E). The remaining 48 species were new records for the Schwoebel tract, as they were not included in the vegetation alliances associated with the tract (Appendix D). Seven species of woody plants documented during the vegetation-mapping project and four species predicted to occur were not detected while surveying vertebrates on the tract (Appendix D).

In the past, the Schwoebel property was managed as a nursery and currently, over two-thirds of the tract contain abandoned nursery trees and shrubs in an early successional stage. Because of the presence of a number of hybrid and cultivated species in abandoned nursery habitat, we identified certain woody plants to the genus level of taxonomic classification (e.g., Austrian-red pine [*Pinus* spp.], magnolia [*Magnolia* spp.], sweet cherry-plum [*Prunus* spp.], and mock-orange [*Philadelphus* spp.]), but were unable to classify the plants to the species level (Appendix D). Location of individual plant species within the tract is available in the Microsoft Access database that accompanies our final report.

Discussion

The objectives of our biotic inventory were to compile a list of all herpetofauna, mammal, bird, and woody plant species and to determine species richness, relative abundance, and distribution of animal species on the Schwoebel tract at VAFO. Even though the property is small (29 ha [72 ac]) and contains only four cover types, we detected 98 species of vertebrates and 78 species of woody plants on the tract.

Herpetofauna

Species richness of herpetofauna detected on the Schwoebel tract between February and October 2004 included four salamander, four anuran, two snake, and one turtle species. None of the herpetofauna detected on the tract was federal or state species of special concern. Several factors, including the small size of the tract, lack of cover type diversity, and a short duration (one year) for the inventory, all contributed to the low number of herpetofauna and lack of species of concern on the site. Additionally, all of the species of herpetofauna detected during our inventory were previously documented at VAFO during the inventory conducted by Tiebout (2003a). Tiebout (2003a) recorded three salamanders (red-spotted newt, northern red and slimy salamanders), four anuran (bullfrog, gray treefrog, wood frog, and Fowler's toad), five turtles (red-eared slider, common map, common musk, common snapping, and eastern painted turtle), and six snakes (eastern milk, northern brown, northern copperhead, northern ring-necked, northern water, and queen snake) that were not detected on the Schwoebel tract. The previous herpetofauna inventory (Tiebout 2003a) of VAFO was conducted for two years and covered a 1,285-ha (3,172-ac) area of park containing 11 cover types, which included the Schuylkill River. In contrast, our one-year inventory was conducted on a 29-ha (72-ac) area that contained four cover types, none of which was unique to the Schwoebel tract. A majority of the herpetofauna species identified during the previous inventory project (Tiebout 2003a) was located within or adjacent to predominant sources of water (Schuylkill River and Valley Creek) that do not occur on the Schwoebel tract. These species ($n = 10$) include red-spotted newt, bullfrog, common map turtle, common musk turtle, common snapping turtle, eastern painted turtle, red-eared slider, northern copperhead, northern water snake, and queen snake.

The Schwoebel tract should be included in any future parkwide, long-term monitoring programs for herpetofauna. As previously recommended by Tiebout (2003a), herpetofauna monitoring on the site should focus on general search (including searching vernal pools) and artificial cover-object transect surveys (incorporating plastic sheets). Even though no egg masses or larvae were detected in vernal pools during 2004, future monitoring of these breeding sites for herpetofauna could possibly indicate the presence of mole salamanders and wood frogs on the site. Because of the lack of aquatic habitat within the tract, we do not recommend conducting basking turtle and anuran-calling surveys on the site. Similar to results of other herpetofauna inventories (Yahner et al. 2001b; Kubel et al. 2002; Tiebout 2003a; Yahner and Ross 2004b), the highest species richness was recorded using general searches (all eight amphibian and the only turtle species). Special emphasis should be directed toward general searches of cover items within or adjacent to Myers Run. All amphibian species and a majority of individual herpetofauna were detected within or in close proximity (< 25 m) to Myers Run. Amphibians can be used as indicators of water quality and the data collected during our inventory serve as a baseline for long-term monitoring of herpetofauna populations associated with Myers Run, a 303[d]-listed, impaired waterway. In addition, the two species of snake were documented using artificial cover objects and as previously recommended and demonstrated (Kjoss and Litvaitis 2001; Kubel et al. 2002; Yahner and Ross 2004b), the highest number of individual snakes was located under plastic sheets. Results of inventorying based on general searches and artificial cover-object transect surveys conducted at our sampling locations provided information on species richness, relative abundance, and distribution of herpetofauna. With future monitoring, results can be compared among years and time periods and to results from this project because of standard survey protocols. Conducting general searches and artificial cover-object surveys will increase the likelihood of incorporating variable weather conditions (i.e., drought, heavy rains), provide the most reliable data, and provide information on long-term trends in herpetofauna populations. Future monitoring of herpetofauna on the Schwoebel tract at VAFO is critical to help determine the impact of natural succession, human influences (i.e., manipulation of vegetation and alteration of cover types by future development), changes in water quality, and inter-specific wildlife impacts (i.e., over-browsing by white-tailed deer) on relative abundance, distribution, and composition of the herpetofauna community on the tract.

Mammals

Between February and October 2004, we detected 14 species of mammals on the Schwoebel tract at VAFO. We did not encounter species that are federally threatened or endangered (USFWS 2005) or special concern in Pennsylvania (PANHP 2006). Therefore, management activities on the Schwoebel tract would not be expected to impact any mammalian species of conservation concern. All species recorded tend to be habitat generalists or edge species and are present within a variety of cover types. Two of the more habitat-specific species (meadow vole and meadow jumping mouse) prefer moist grasslands or old field habitat with lush vegetative ground cover (Merritt 1987). However, like many of the other species detected on the tract, these two species can occupy a variety of early successional and edge habitats containing herbaceous-ground vegetation. Even though no comprehensive inventory of mammals has been conducted at the park, we added only one new species record to the list of mammals documented at VAFO. Although mammal survey work has been done in the past (Yahner et al. 1997) and was conducted at VAFO concurrent to the Schwoebel inventory (Yahner et al. 2006a, 2006b), we recorded the first weasel (probably long-tailed weasel) at the park during our inventory of the Schwoebel tract. The tract contains all of the characteristics considered to be optimal habitat for weasels, including open woodlands with dense, brushy thickets in close proximity to water (Merritt 1987). Two possible reasons why weasels have not been documented previously at VAFO are because of their nocturnal activity and because no comprehensive inventory of mammals has been conducted at the park.

Several factors contributed to the low species richness of mammals and lack of species of concern on the Schwoebel tract. As previously mentioned, the tract is small and contains little habitat diversity, and our inventory consisted of a single year snapshot of the area. A number of ubiquitous, habitat generalist species, either documented previously at VAFO or predicted to occur on the tract, was not detected during 2004. We expected to locate eastern chipmunk and southern red-backed vole, two species of mammals that occur in many successional stages and types of forests (Merritt 1987). Neither of these species was found on the tract, possibly because of a lack of vegetative cover at the forest floor accompanied by a lack of downed woody debris, stumps, and rotting logs. Additionally, the tract did not provide optimal habitat for red squirrel, defined as closed canopy, mature eastern hemlock and white pine forest.

We recommend further inventory and subsequent monitoring of mammals on the Schwoebel tract to increase the likelihood of incorporating variability or to determine changes in the mammal community based on biotic (microtine cycles, overbrowsing of vegetation by white-tailed deer) and abiotic (weather) factors that cannot be measured during a one-year study.

Based on results from the inventory, concurrent projects (Yahner et al. 2006a, 2006b), and past protocol and inventory work (Yahner et al. 1997; Yahner et al. 2004a), mammal work on the site should center on (1) live-trapping surveys incorporating many different sized traps for small (Norway rat and smaller) and medium-sized mammals (Norway rat to common raccoon) and (2) opportunistic observations to target mammals larger than Norway rat. Although we identified only four mammal species using live-trapping surveys, we recommend further live-trapping because handling and close examination of live and dead captures is necessary to identify small mammals (e.g., voles, mice, shrews) to the species level of taxonomic classification. Because of the small amount of paved, secondary roads on the site (< 0.5 km), lack of total area that can be covered by a vehicular-road survey, and limited results from our spotlighting surveys, we do not recommend using spotlighting or vehicular-road protocols to survey mammals on the Schwoebel tract.

Birds

Similar to bird inventories conducted at other parks in Pennsylvania (Yahner et al. 2001a; Yahner et al. 2004a), we detected the highest number of bird species ($n = 41$) during the spring-migratory season. The total number of species found on the tract ($n = 73$) was lower than the number recorded at VAFO during the most recent bird inventory ($n = 163$), and all species detected on the tract were recorded during the recent inventory of VAFO (Yahner et al 2001a). Size and number of different habitats present within VAFO (1,314 ha and 11 cover types) versus the Schwoebel tract (29 ha and four cover types) and duration of the two inventories (Yahner et al. 2001a was two years and our inventory was one year) contributed to the discrepancy between number of species recorded previously at VAFO versus number of species observed on the Schwoebel tract. Similar to comparisons of herpetofauna inventories, the previous bird inventory of VAFO was conducted for two years and covered a 1,285-ha (3,172-ac) area of park that contained 11 cover types compared to a one-year bird inventory conducted on 29 ha (72 ac) containing four cover type classifications, all of which are present in VAFO. However, species richness of birds on the Schwoebel tract was what we expected for a 29-ha (72-acre) area that contained seven point-count sampling points. Species richness on the Schwoebel tract was comparable to that of Johnstown Flood National Memorial, a park similar in size (63 ha [156 ac]) and containing a similar number of point-count sampling points ($n = 10$) (Yahner et al 2001a).

Although the Schwoebel tract contains no unique cover-type classifications, when combined with the extensive area under federal ownership at VAFO, the tract serves as an important location for bird conservation in southeastern Pennsylvania. Most notably, seven species of special concern used the tract, including four possible breeders (American woodcock, willow flycatcher, wood thrush [third most abundant species on the tract during the breeding season], and Louisiana waterthrush). Four of the seven species, including American woodcock, willow flycatcher, blue-winged warbler, and prairie warbler, are associated with early successional or old-field habitat (Brauning 1992). Additionally, wood thrush and black-billed cuckoo are associated with forested areas containing a well-developed understory of shrubs and saplings. With the increasing loss of early successional habitat to development (Yahner 2000) and the majority of Pennsylvania forests being even-aged, mature stands (80–120 yrs) (Bureau of Forestry, PA DCNR and USDA Forest Service 2004), maintenance and management of grassland/old-field and early successional forest habitats similar to those present on the Schwoebel tract will benefit bird species of concern requiring these habitats. However, with less than one percent of the 29 ha (72 ac) classified as mature forest, we were not surprised to detect only one species of owl (identified from owl pellets) on the tract.

We recommend further inventory and subsequent monitoring of birds on the Schwoebel tract. Based on results from our project and past protocol and inventory work (Yahner et al. 2001a; Yahner et al. 2004a), we recommend continuing bird point-count surveys on the site. Results from point-count surveys will provide information on bird species richness and relative abundance that can be compared to results from previous bird research conducted at VAFO (Yahner et al. 2001a). Although we were unable to detect owls using taped-playback surveys during 2004, the nocturnal-owl survey protocol is the only survey method that provides an accurate estimate of species richness and relative abundance for owls and should be included in a bird-monitoring program. Other survey methods fail to detect and tend to underestimate the abundance of these species because owls are inconspicuous and rarely vocalize during the day. Combinations of point-count and owl surveys provide the most reliable data and provide information on long-term trends in bird populations. Future monitoring of avian populations is critical to help determine the impact of natural succession and human influences (i.e., development and/or building renovation) on bird-community composition at the tract. Continued monitoring of birds likely will result in documentation of additional species that are typical of old field and early successional forested habitat.

Woody Plants

The vegetation alliances or cover types on the Schwoebel tract reflect land-use history, lack of recent management, and low diversity of vegetation alliances on the site. The majority (67 %) of the tract is composed of abandoned shrub and tree nursery interspersed with travel corridors and abandoned buildings and a small amount of grassland and old field or successional forest. Although vegetation mapping and habitat classification were conducted recently at VAFO (including the Schwoebel tract) (Lundgren et al. 2002), the project was not intended to be a comprehensive inventory of woody plants throughout the park. Despite not conducting a formal inventory of woody plant species, we supplemented the list of woody plant species identified on the tract using opportunistic observations to detect 48 woody plant species not documented previously or predicted to occur on the site by the vegetation-mapping project. Although we provided thorough coverage of and multiple visits to the tract during 2004, we failed to detect 11 species of woody plants associated with vegetation alliances.

In addition to the lack of a comprehensive inventory of woody plants on the tract, no formal inventory of herbaceous vegetation was conducted during our project or the vegetation-mapping project. Therefore, we recommend conducting a detailed inventory of both woody and herbaceous plants to determine relative abundance and distribution of plant species, as well as identifying additional species not previously documented on the Schwoebel tract.

Conclusions

National parks are becoming more insular because of increased habitat fragmentation in the surrounding landscape, making these parks valuable for the long-term maintenance of biological diversity. The National Park Service has determined the need to inventory amphibian, reptile, mammal, bird, and woody plant species on the Schwoebel tract (acquired in August 2004) to complement recently conducted inventories of herpetofauna (Tiebout 2003a; Yahner et al 2006a), mammals (Yahner et al. 2006a, 2006b), birds (Yahner et al. 2001a), and vegetation (Lundgren et al. 2002) at VAFO. The objectives of our inventory in 2004 were to document (1) presence, relative abundance, and distribution of herpetofauna, mammals, and birds on the Schwoebel tract and (2) presence of woody plant species on the Schwoebel tract.

We surveyed herpetofauna on the Schwoebel tract at VAFO between 9 February–28 October 2004 using opportunistic observations and general search, anuran-calling, and artificial cover-object transect surveys. Four salamander, four anuran, one turtle, and two snake species were detected on the tract, and all herpetofauna were species documented previously at VAFO. We inventoried mammals using opportunistic observations and live-trapping and spotlighting surveys. Fourteen species of mammals were observed on the tract, with only a species of weasel (probably long-tailed weasel) not documented previously at VAFO. Bird populations were surveyed during spring-migratory, breeding, fall-migratory, and winter seasons using opportunistic observations, point-count, and owl surveys. We documented 73 bird species, including seven species listed federally as birds of conservation concern and/or Audubon WatchList species. We also documented 78 woody plant species using opportunistic observations, including 48 species that were not included in the vegetation alliances used to describe the Schwoebel tract during the most recent vegetation-mapping project conducted at VAFO (Lundgren et al. 2002). Although the Schwoebel tract is small (29 ha [72 ac]), contains relatively few cover types ($n = 4$), and our inventory was conducted for one year, we were able to detect 98 species of vertebrates. Further inventorying and monitoring of flora and fauna likely will continue to increase the number of species observed on the Schwoebel tract.

In conjunction with recently conducted herpetofauna, mammal, and bird inventories and vegetation mapping at VAFO, information acquired during our inventory of the Schwoebel tract will establish the foundation for a database of flora and fauna at the park. By developing a monitoring program based on survey protocols and locations from recently conducted inventory projects, resource management specialists can create an extensive, long-term database of flora and fauna while adding to information already accumulated on presence, relative abundance, and distribution of species within VAFO. Based on knowledge and information derived from this database, resource management specialists will be able to make informed decisions on how best to manage natural resources within the national parks.

Literature Cited

Ambrose, J. P., and S. P. Bratton. 1990. Trends in landscape heterogeneity along the borders of Great Smoky Mountains National Park. Conservation Biology 4.

Brauning, D. W. 1992. Atlas of breeding birds in Pennsylvania. University of Pittsburgh Press. Pittsburgh, PA.

Bureau of Forestry, PA DCNR, and USDA Forest Service. 2004. The state of the forest: a snapshot of Pennsylvania's updated forest inventory 2004. PA DCNR Bureau of Forestry. Harrisburg, PA.

Burt, W. H., and R. P. Grossenheider. 1980. A field guide to the mammals: North America north of Mexico. Third edition. Houghton Mifflin Company. Boston, MA.

Buskirk, W., and J. L. McDonald. 1995. Comparison of point count sampling regimes for monitoring forest birds. General Technical Report PSW-GTR 149. USDA Forest Service. Albany, CA.

Carfioli, M. A. 1998. Inventorying and monitoring herpetofaunal populations using coverboards as artificial refugia at Valley Forge National Historical Park. Final Report, Internship in Biological Sciences (BIO 409). West Chester University. West Chester, PA.

Carfioli, M. A. 2000. Influence of coverboard design on microclimate conditions and herpetofaunal patterns of use. M.S. Thesis. West Chester University.

Cypher, E. A., R. H. Yahner, G. L. Storm, and B. L. Cypher. 1985. Valley Forge National Historical Park proposed Pawling Recreation Area flora and fauna survey. Final Report, Contract No. 14-16-0009-1548. National Park Service. Philadelphia, PA.

Dawson, K. D., D. R. Smith, and C. S. Robbins. 1995. Point count length and detection of forest Neotropical migrant birds. General Technical Report PSW-GTR 149. USDA Forest Service. Albany, CA.

DeGraaf, R. M., and M. Yamasaki. 1992. A nondestructive technique to monitor the relative abundance of terrestrial salamanders. Wildlife Society Bulletin 20.

Droege, S., L. Monti, and D. Lantz. 1997. The Terrestrial Salamander Monitoring Program: recommended protocol for running cover object arrays. United States Department of the Interior, U.S. Geological Survey, Patuxent Wildlife Research Center. Laurel, MD. http://www.pwrc.usgs.gov/Sally/sally4.html.

Environmental Systems Research Institute, Inc. (ESRI). 2000. ArcView GIS Version 3.2a. Environmental Systems Research Institute, Inc. Redlands, CA.

Fitch, H. S. 1992. Protocols of sampling snake populations and their relative success. Herpetological Review 23.

Foster, F. 1965. An early reference of the technique of owl calling. Auk 82.

Fuller, R. J., and D. R. Langslow. 1984. Estimating numbers of birds by point counts: How long should counts last. Bird Study 31.

Grossman, D. H., D. Faber-Langendoen, A. S. Weakley, M. Anderson, P. Bourgeron, R. Crawford, K. Goodin, S. Landaal, K. Metzler, K. Patterson, and others. 1998. International classification of ecological communities: terrestrial vegetation of the United States. Volume 1. The National Vegetation Classification System: development, status, and applications. The Nature Conservancy. Arlington, VA.

Hutto, R. L., S. M. Pletschet, and P. Hendricks. 1986. A fixed-radius point count method for nonbreeding and breeding season use. Auk 103.

International Bird Census Committee (IBCC). 1977. Censusing breeding birds by the IPA method. Polish Ecological Studies 3.

Kjoss, V. A., and J. A. Litvaitis. 2001. Comparison of 2 methods to sample snake communities in early successional habitats. Wildlife Society Bulletin 29.

Kubel, J. E., K. L. Derge, J. Williams, and R. H. Yahner. 2002. Amphibian and reptile inventory at Antietam National Battlefield, Maryland. Maryland Naturalist 45.

Lundgren, J., G. Podniesinski, and L. Sneddon. 2002. NPS Vegetation Mapping Program: vegetation classification of Valley Forge National Historical Park. Draft Final Report. National Park Service. Philadelphia, PA.

Lutcher, F. C. 1996. Surveying herpetofaunal diversity using artificial refugia: a comparison of coverboard designs. Final Report, Internship in Biological Sciences (BIO 409). West Chester University. West Chester, PA.

Lynch, P. J., and D. G. Smith. 1984. Census of eastern screech-owls (*Otus asio*) in urban open-space areas using tape-recorded calls. American Birds 38.

Merritt, J. F. 1987. Guide to the mammals of Pennsylvania. University of Pittsburgh Press, Pittsburgh, PA.

Morrell, T. E. 1993. Status and habitat characteristics of the great horned owl in south central Pennsylvania. Ph.D. Dissertation. The Pennsylvania State University, University Park.

National Park Service (NPS). 2000. Natural resource inventory and monitoring in national parks. NPS Inventory and Monitoring Program informational brochure. http://www1.nature.nps.gov/im/brochure/imbroch.htm

National Park Service (NPS). 2003. Inventory and monitoring program: NPSpecies home page. http://science.nature.nps.gov/im/apps/npspp/index.htm

National Park Service (NPS). October 2004. NPSpecies - The National Park Service species database. Version 2.1. http://science.nature.nps.gov/npspecies (password protected). Information page, http://www.nature.nps.gov/im/apps/npspp.index.htm.

Pennsylvania Natural Heritage Program (PANHP). 2006. Vertebrate species [of special concern] list. http://www.naturalheritage.state.pa.us/vertebrates.aspx.

Petranka, J. W. 1998. Salamanders of the United States and Canada. Smithsonian Institution Press, Washington, D.C.

Savard, J-P. L., and T. D. Hooper. 1995. Influence of survey length and radius size on grassland bird surveys by point counts at Williams Lake, British Columbia. General Technical Report PSW-GTR 149. USDA Forest Service. Albany, CA.

Shaffer, L. L. 1991. Pennsylvania amphibians and reptiles. Pennsylvania Fish and Boat Commission Bureau of Education and Information. Harrisburg, Pennsylvania.

Tiebout III, H. M. 2003a. An inventory of the herpetofauna of Valley Forge National Historical Park. Technical Report NPS/PHSO/NRTR-03/088. National Park Service. Philadelphia, PA.

Tiebout III, H. M. 2003b. Herpetofauna survey handbook: inventory and monitoring data collection methods for Valley Forge National Historical Park. Report, Cooperative Agreement 4000-9-9016. National Park Service. Philadelphia, PA.

United States Fish and Wildlife Service (USFWS). 2005. Species information: threatened and endangered animals and plants. http://endangered.fws.gov/wildlife.html.

Verner, J., and L. V. Ritter. 1986. Hourly variation in morning point counts of birds. Auk 103.

Yahner, R. H., G. L. Storm, G. S. Keller, B. D. Ross, and R. W. Rohrbaugh, Jr. 1997. Inventorying and monitoring protocols of mammals in national parks of the eastern United States. Technical Report NPS/PHSO/NRTR-97/073. National Park Service. Philadelphia, PA.

Yahner, R. H., G. L. Storm, G. S. Keller, B. D. Ross, and R. W. Rohrbaugh, Jr. 1999. Inventorying and monitoring protocols of amphibians and reptiles in national parks of the eastern United States. Technical Report NPS/PHSO/NRTR-99/076. National Park Service. Philadelphia, PA.

Yahner, R. H. 2000. Eastern deciduous forest: ecology and wildlife conservation. Second edition. University of Minnesota Press. Minneapolis, MN.

Yahner, R. H., B. D. Ross, G. S. Keller, and D. S. Klute. 2001a. Comprehensive inventory program for birds at six Pennsylvania national parks. Technical Report NPS/PHSO/NRTR-01/085. National Park Service. Philadelphia, PA.

Yahner, R. H., K. L. Derge, and J. Mravintz. 2001b. Inventory of amphibian and reptile species at Gettysburg National Military Park and Eisenhower National Historic Site. Technical Report NPS/PHSO/NRTR-01/084. National Park Service. Philadelphia, PA.

Yahner, R. H., J. E. Kubel, K. L. Derge, and J. Williams. 2002. Inventory of amphibians and reptiles at Antietam National Battlefield, Maryland. Final Report, Cooperative Agreement 4000-8-9028, Supplemental Agreement No. 4. National Park Service. Philadelphia, PA.

Yahner, R. H., B. D. Ross, and J. E. Kubel. 2004a. Comprehensive inventory of birds and mammals at Fort Necessity National Battlefield and Friendship Hill National Historic Site. Technical Report NPS/NERCHAL/NRTR-04/093. National Park Service. Philadelphia, PA.

Yahner, R. H., and B. D. Ross. 2004b. Comprehensive inventory of amphibians, reptiles, and mammals at Allegheny Portage Railroad National Historic Site and Johnstown Flood National Memorial. Annual Progress Report, Cooperative Agreement No. 4000-8-9028, Supplemental Agreement No. 22. National Park Service. Philadelphia, PA.

Yahner, R. H., J. E. Kubel, and B. D. Ross. 2006a. Inventory of herpetofauna and small mammals in the Asbestos Release Site Areas of Concern at Valley Forge National Historical Park. Technical Report NPS/NER/NRTR—2006/069. National Park Service. Philadelphia, PA.

Yahner, R. H., J. E. Kubel, and B. D. Ross. 2006b. Inventory of mammals at Valley Forge National Historical Park. Technical Report NPS/NER/NRTR—2006/070. National Park Service. Philadelphia, PA.

Appendix A. Herpetofauna species previously documented, predicted to occur, and/or inventoried during 2004 on the Schwoebel tract at Valley Forge National Historical Park (VAFO), Pennsylvania.

Common Name	Scientific Name	Doc./Pred.[a]	Inv.[b]
Salamanders:			
longtail salamander	*Eurycea l. longicauda*	D	I
northern dusky salamander	*Desmognathus f. fuscus*	D	I
northern red salamander	*Pseudotriton r. ruber*	D	
slimy salamander	*Plethodon glutinosus*	D	
northern two-lined salamander	*Eurycea b. bislineata*	D	I
redback salamander	*Plethodon cinereus*	D	I
red-spotted newt	*Notophthalmus v. viridescens*	D	
Toads and Frogs:			
bullfrog	*Rana catesbeiana*	D	
eastern American toad	*Bufo a. americanus*	D	I
eastern spadefoot	*Scaphiopus h. holbrookii*	P	
Fowler's toad	*Bufo woodhousii fowleri*	D	
gray treefrog	*Hyla versicolor*	D	
green frog	*Rana clamitans melanota*	D	I
northern leopard frog	*Rana pipiens*	P	
northern spring peeper	*Pseudacris c. crucifer*	D	I
pickerel frog	*Rana palustris*	D	I
wood frog	*Rana sylvatica*	D	
Turtles:			
common map turtle	*Graptemys geographica*	DNP	
common musk turtle	*Sternotherus odoratus*	DNP	
common snapping turtle	*Chelydra s. serpentina*	DNP	
eastern box turtle	*Terrapene c. carolina*	D	I
eastern painted turtle	*Chrysemys p. picta*	DNP	
midland painted turtle	*Chrysemys picta marginata*	DNP/P	
redbelly turtle	*Pseudemys rubriventris*	DNP/P	
red-eared slider	*Trachemys scripta elegans*	DNP	
spotted turtle	*Clemmys guttata*	DNP	
Snakes:			
black rat snake	*Elaphe o. obsoleta*	P	
eastern garter snake	*Thamnophis s. sirtalis*	D	I
eastern milk snake	*Lampropeltis t. triangulum*	D	
eastern worm snake	*Carphophis a. amoenus*	P	
northern black racer	*Coluber c. constrictor*	D	I
northern brown snake	*Storeria d. dekayi*	D	
northern copperhead	*Agkistrodon contortrix mokasen*	D	
northern ringneck snake	*Diadophis punctatus edwardsii*	D	
northern water snake	*Nerodia s. sipedon*	D	
queen snake	*Regina septemvittata*	D	

[a]Documented or predicted: D = documented at VAFO as recently as 1999 during the most recent inventory of herpetofauna (Tiebout 2003a) and predicted to occur on the Schwoebel tract; DNP/P = not documented during the most recent inventory (Tiebout 2003a), but documented previously at VAFO (Cypher et al. 1985), but not predicted due to lack of suitable habitat; P = never documented at VAFO, but classified as "probably present" in the NPSpecies database (National Park Service 2004) and, therefore, predicted to occur on the Schwoebel tract; DNP = documented at VAFO as recently as 1999 during the most recent inventory of herpetofauna (Tiebout 2003a), but not predicted to occur on the Schwoebel tract due to lack of suitable aquatic habitat.
[b]Inventoried: I = recorded on the Schwoebel tract February–October, 2004.

Appendix B. Mammalian species previously documented, predicted to occur, and/or inventoried during 2004 on the Schwoebel tract at Valley Forge National Historical Park (VAFO), Pennsylvania.

Common Name[a]	Scientific Name	Doc./Pred.[b]	Inv.[c]
Opossum:			
Virginia opossum	*Didelphis virginiana*	D	I
Shrews:			
masked shrew	*Sorex cinereus*	D	I
smoky shrew	*Sorex fumeus*	PNS	
northern short-tailed shrew	*Blarina brevicauda kirtlandi*	D	I
least shrew	*Cryptotis parva*	P	
Moles:			
hairy-tailed mole	*Parascalops breweri*	P	
eastern mole	*Scalopus aquaticus*	P	
star-nosed mole	*Condylura cristata*	D	
Rabbits:			
eastern cottontail	*Sylvilagus floridanus*	D	I
Appalacian cottontail	*Sylvilagus obscurus*	PNS	
Squirrels:			
eastern chipmunk	*Tamias striatus*	D	
woodchuck	*Marmota monax*	D	I
eastern gray squirrel	*Sciurus carolinensis*	D	I
eastern fox squirrel	*Sciurus niger*	P	
Squirrels (continued):			
red squirrel	*Tamiasciurus hudsonicus*	D	
southern flying squirrel	*Glaucomys volans*	D	
Beaver:			
beaver	*Castor canadensis*	PNS	
New world mice, and voles:			
deer mouse	*Peromyscus maniculatus bairdii*	D	
white-footed mouse	*Peromyscus leucopus*	D	I
southern red-backed vole	*Clethrionomys gapperi*	P	
meadow vole	*Microtus pennsylvanicus*	D	I
pine vole	*Microtus pinetorum*	P	
southern bog lemming	*Synaptomys cooperi*	PNS	
muskrat	*Ondatra zibethicus*	D	
Old world rat and mouse:			
Norway rat	*Rattus norvegicus*	D	
house mouse	*Mus musculus*	D	
Jumping mouse:			
meadow jumping mouse	*Zapus hudsonius*	D	I
Dog and Foxes:			
coyote	*Canis latrans*	P	
red fox	*Vulpes vulpes*	D	I
gray fox	*Urocyon cinereoargenteus*	P	
Raccoon:			
common raccoon	*Procyon lotor*	D	I

Appendix B. Mammalian species previously documented, predicted to occur, and/or inventoried during 2004 on the Schwoebel tract at Valley Forge National Historical Park (VAFO), Pennsylvania (continued).

Common Name[a]	Scientific Name	Doc./Pred.[b]	Inv.[c]
Weasels:			
long-tailed weasel [d]	*Mustela frenata*	P	I
ermine [d]	*Mustela erminea*	P	I
mink	*Mustela vison*	PNS	
striped skunk	*Mephitis mephitis*	D	
Cat:			
domestic cat	*Felis catus*	D	I
Deer:			
white-tailed deer	*Odocoileus virginianus*	D	I

[a]Identification of bat species requires specialized training and an intensive sampling effort, so we did not sample for bat species during the inventory.

[b]Documented or predicted: D = documented at VAFO (all mammal records for the park that are currently in the NPSpecies database are classified as "present," having been documented as recently as 1979); P = never documented at VAFO, but range maps (Burt and Grossenheider 1980; Merritt 1987) indicate possible presence and, therefore, species is predicted; PNS = never documented at VAFO. Range maps (Burt and Grossenheider 1980; Merritt 1987) indicate possible presence at VAFO, but not predicted to occur on the Schwoebel tract due to lack of suitable habitat.

[c]Inventoried: I = recorded on the Schwoebel tract February–October, 2004.

[d]An opportunistic observation was made of an individual that could not be differentiated between long-tailed weasel and ermine.

Appendix C. Bird species previously documented, predicted to occur, and/or inventoried during 2004 on the Schwoebel tract at Valley Forge National Historical Park (VAFO), Pennsylvania.

Common Name[a]	Scientific Name	Doc./Pred.[b]	Inv.[c]
Goose:			
Canada goose	*Branta canadensis*	D	I
New world vultures:			
turkey vulture	*Cathartes aura*	D	I
black vulture	*Coragyps atratus*	D	I
Eagle and Hawks:			
northern harrier	*Circus cyaneus*	D	
golden eagle	*Aquila chrysaetos*	D	
sharp-shinned hawk	*Accipiter striatus*	D	
Cooper's hawk	*Accipiter cooperii*	D	I
broad-winged hawk	*Buteo platypterus*	D	
red-shouldered hawk	*Buteo lineatus*	D	I
red-tailed hawk	*Buteo jamaicensis*	D	I
Falcon:			
American kestrel	*Falco sparverius*	D	
Pheasant:			
ring-necked pheasant	*Phasianus colchicus*	D	
Plover:			
killdeer	*Charadrius vociferus*	D	
Sandpiper:			
American woodcock	*Scolopax minor*	D	I
Gull:			
herring gull	*Larus argentatus*	D	I
Doves:			
rock dove	*Columba livia*	D	I
mourning dove	*Zenaida macroura*	D	I
Cuckoos:			
yellow-billed cuckoo	*Coccyzus americanus*	D	
black-billed cuckoo	*Coccyzus erythropthalmus*	D	I
Owls:			
barn owl	*Tyota alba*	P	
great horned owl	*Bubo virginianus*	D	I
long-eared owl	*Asio otus*	D	
barred owl	*Strix varia*	D	
eastern screech-owl	*Otus asio*	D	
northern saw-whet owl	*Aegolius acadicus*	D	
Nighthawk and Nightjar:			
common nighthawk	*Chordeiles minor*	D	
whip-poor-will	*Caprimulgus vociferus*	D/P	
Swift:			
chimney swift	*Chaetura pelagica*	D	I
Hummingbird:			
ruby-throated hummingbird	*Archilochus colubris*	D	
Kingfishers:			
belted kingfisher	*Ceryle alcyon*	D	

Appendix C. Bird species previously documented, predicted to occur, and/or inventoried during 2004 on the Schwoebel tract at Valley Forge National Historical Park (VAFO), Pennsylvania (continued).

Common Name[a]	Scientific Name	Doc./Pred.[b]	Inv.[c]
Woodpeckers:			
red-headed woodpecker	*Melanerpes erythrocephalus*	D	
red-bellied woodpecker	*Melanerpes carolinus*	D	I
northern flicker	*Colaptes auratus*	D	I
yellow-bellied sapsucker	*Sphyrapicus varius*	D	
downy woodpecker	*Picoides pubescens*	D	I
hairy woodpecker	*Picoides villosus*	D	I
pileated woodpecker	*Dryocopus pileatus*	D	
Tyrant flycatchers:			
eastern wood-pewee	*Contopus virens*	D	
acadian flycatcher	*Empidonax virescens*	D	
yellow-bellied flycatcher	*Empidonax flaviventris*	D	
alder flycatcher	*Empidonax alnorum*	D	
willow flycatcher	*Empidonax traillii*	D	I
least flycatcher	*Empidonax minimus*	D	
great crested flycatcher	*Myiarchus crinitus*	D	
eastern kingbird	*Tyrannus tyrannus*	D	
Vireos:			
white-eyed vireo	*Vireo griseus*	D	I
yellow-throated vireo	*Vireo flavifrons*	D	
blue-headed vireo	*Vireo solitarius*	D	I
red-eyed vireo	*Vireo olivaceus*	D	I
Philadelphia vireo	*Vireo philadelphicus*	D	
warbling vireo	*Vireo gilvus*	D	
Jay and Crows:			
blue jay	*Cyanocitta cristata*	D	I
American crow	*Corvus brachyrhynchos*	D	I
fish crow	*Corvus ossifragus*	D	
common raven	*Corvus corax*	D	
Lark:			
horned lark	*Eremophila alpestris*	D	
Swallows:			
tree swallow	*Tachycineta bicolor*	D	I
barn swallow	*Hirundo rustica*	D	
Titmouse and Chickadee:			
tufted titmouse	*Baeolophus bicolor*	D	I
Carolina chickadee	*Poecile carolinensis*	D	I
Creeper:			
brown creeper	*Certhia americana*	D	
Nuthatches:			
white-breasted nuthatch	*Sitta carolinensis*	D	I
red-breasted nuthatch	*Sitta canadensis*	D	

Appendix C. Bird species previously documented, predicted to occur, and/or inventoried during 2004 on the Schwoebel tract at Valley Forge National Historical Park (VAFO), Pennsylvania (continued).

Common Name[a]	Scientific Name	Doc./Pred.[b]	Inv.[c]
Wrens:			
house wren	*Troglodytes aedon*	D	I
winter wren	*Troglodytes troglodytes*	D	
Carolina wren	*Thyothorus ludovicianus*	D	I
marsh wren	*Cistothorus palustris*	D	
Kinglets:			
golden-crowned kinglet	*Regulus satrapa*	D	I
ruby-crowned kinglet	*Regulus calendula*	D	I
Gnatcatcher:			
blue-gray gnatcatcher	*Polioptila caerulea*	D	I
Thrushes:			
eastern bluebird	*Sialia sialis*	D	I
wood thrush	*Hylocichla mustelina*	D	I
veery	*Catharus fuscescens*	D	I
gray-cheeked thrush	*Catharus minimus*	D	
Swainson's thrush	*Catharus ustulatus*	D	
hermit thrush	*Catharus guttatus*	D	
American robin	*Turdus migratorius*	D	I
Mockingbirds and Thrasher:			
gray catbird	*Dumetella carolinensis*	D	I
northern mockingbird	*Mimus polyglottos*	D	I
brown thrasher	*Toxostoma rufum*	D	I
Starling:			
European starling	*Sturnus vulgaris*	D	I
Waxwing:			
cedar waxwing	*Bombycilla cedrorum*	D	I
Wood-warblers:			
blue-winged warbler	*Vermivora pinus*	D	I
Tennessee warbler	*Vermivora peregrina*	D	
Nashville warbler	*Vermivora ruficapilla*	D	I
northern parula	*Parula americana*	D	
chestnut-sided warbler	*Dendroica pensylvanica*	D	I
Cape May warbler	*Dendroica tigrina*	D	
magnolia warbler	*Dendroica magnolia*	D	I
yellow-rumped warbler	*Dendroic coronata*	D	I
black-and-white warbler	*Mniotilta varia*	D	I
black-throated blue warbler	*Dendroica caerulescens*	D	
cerulean warbler	*Dendroica cerulea*	D	
blackburnian warbler	*Dendroica fusca*	D	
black-throated green warbler	*Dendroica virens*	D	I
yellow-throated warbler	*Dendroica dominica*	D/P	
prairie warbler	*Dendroica discolor*	D	I
bay-breasted warbler	*Dendroica castanea*	D	
blackpoll warbler	*Dendroica striata*	D	I

43

Appendix C. Bird species previously documented, predicted to occur, and/or inventoried during 2004 on the Schwoebel tract at Valley Forge National Historical Park (VAFO), Pennsylvania (continued).

Common Name[a]	Scientific Name	Doc./Pred.[b]	Inv.[c]
Wood-warblers (continued):			
pine warbler	*Dendroica pinus*	D	
palm warbler	*Dendroica palmarum*	D	I
yellow warbler	*Dendroica petechia*	D	I
Kentucky warbler	*Oporornis formosus*	D	
Canada warbler	*Wilsonia canadensis*	D	
Wilson's warbler	*Wilsonia pusilla*	D	
hooded warbler	*Wilsonia citrina*	D	
worm-eating warbler	*Helmitheros vermivorus*	D	
ovenbird	*Seiurus aurocapillus*	D	
Louisiana waterthrush	*Seiurus motacilla*	D	I
northern waterthrush	*Seiurus noveboracensis*	D	I
common yellowthroat	*Geothlypis trichas*	D	I
American redstart	*Setophaga ruticilla*	D	I
Tanager:			
scarlet tanager	*Piranga olivacea*	D	
Emberizids:			
eastern towhee	*Pipilo erythrophthalmus*	D	I
American tree sparrow	*Spizella arborea*	D	I
field sparrow	*Spizella pusilla*	D	I
chipping sparrow	*Spizella passerina*	D	
grasshopper sparrow	*Ammodramus savannarum*	D	
fox sparrow	*Passerella iliaca*	D	
savannah sparrow	*Passerculus sandwichensis*	D	
Lincoln's sparrow	*Melospiza lincolnii*	D	
song sparrow	*Melospiza melodia*	D	I
vesper sparrow	*Pooecetes gramineus*	D	
swamp sparrow	*Melospiza georgiana*	D	
white-throated sparrow	*Zonotrichia albicollis*	D	I
dark-eyed junco	*Junco hyemalis*	D	I
Cardinals:			
rose-breasted grosbeak	*Pheucticus ludovicianus*	D	I
northern cardinal	*Cardinalis cardinalis*	D	I
blue grosbeak	*Guiraca caerulea*	D	
indigo bunting	*Passerina cyanea*	D	
Blackbirds:			
bobolink	*Dolichonyx oryzivorus*	D	I
eastern meadowlark	*Sturnella magna*	D	
red-winged blackbird	*Agelaius phoeniceus*	D	I
common grackle	*Quiscalus quiscula*	D	I
brown-headed cowbird	*Molothrus ater*	D	I
orchard oriole	*Icterus spurius*	D	
Baltimore oriole	*Icterus galbula*	D	I

Appendix C. Bird species previously documented, predicted to occur, and/or inventoried during 2004 on the Schwoebel tract at Valley Forge National Historical Park (VAFO), Pennsylvania (continued).

Common Name[a]	Scientific Name	Doc./Pred.[b]	Inv.[c]
Finches:			
purple finch	*Carpodacus purpureus*	D	I
house finch	*Carpodacus mexicanus*	D	I
American goldfinch	*Carduelis tristis*	D	I
common redpoll	*Carduelis flammea*	D/P	
Old world sparrow:			
house sparrow	*Passer domesticus*	D	

[a]Waterfowl, shorebirds, and wetland associates were excluded because the Schwoebel tract does not contain substantial aquatic habitat. A majority of the waterfowl, shorebirds, and wetland associates documented by Yahner et al. (2001a) were observed on or in habitat associated with the Schuylkill River.
[b]Documented or predicted: D = documented at VAFO during the most recent inventory by Yahner et al. (2001a); D/P = not documented at VAFO during the most recent inventory by Yahner et al. (2001a), but classified as "present" (documented) in the NPSpecies database (National Park Service 2004) and, therefore, predicted; P = not documented at VAFO during the most recent inventory by Yahner et al. (2001a), but predicted based on range maps and the presence of appropriate habitat (Brauning 1992).
[c]Inventoried: I = recorded on the Schwoebel tract February–October, 2004.

Appendix D. Woody plant species associated with vegetation alliances, predicted to occur, and/or inventoried during 2004 on the Schwoebel tract at Valley Forge National Historical Park (VAFO), Pennsylvania.

Common Name[a]	Scientific Name	Doc./Pred.[b]	Inv.[c]
Pine Family:			
Norway spruce	*Picea abies*		I
Colorado blue spruce	*Picea pungens*		I
red spruce	*Picea rubens*		I
Austrian or red pine	*Pinus nigra* or *P. resinosa* or hybrid		I
eastern white pine	*Pinus strobus*		I
eastern hemlock	*Tsuga canadensis*		I
Cypress Family:			
arbor-vitae	*Thuja occidentalis*		I
Yew Family:			
American yew	*Taxus canadensis*		I
Magnolia Family:			
tuliptree	*Liriodendron tulipifera*	D	I
magnolia (cultivated)	*Magnolia* spp.		I
Laurel Family:			
spicebush	*Lindera benzoin*	D	I
sassafras	*Sassafras albidum*	D	I
Planetree Family:			
sycamore	*Platanus occidentalis*		I
Witch-hazel Family:			
witch-hazel	*Hamamelis virginiana*	P	I
sweet-gum	*Liquidambar styraciflua*		I
Elm Family:			
hackberry	*Celtis occidentalis*		I
American elm	*Ulmus americana*	D	I
Mulberry Family:			
mulberry	*Morus* spp.		I
Walnut Family:			
shagbark hickory	*Carya ovata*	P	I
mockernut hickory	*Carya tomentosa*		I
black walnut	*Juglans nigra*	D	I
Beech Family:			
American chestnut	*Castanea dentata*	P	
American beech	*Fagus grandifolia*	P	I
white oak	*Quercus alba*	P	I
scarlet oak	*Quercus coccinea*	P	
shingle oak	*Quercus imbricaria*		I
pin oak	*Quercus palustris*		I
northern red oak	*Quercus rubra*	D	I
black oak	*Quercus velutina*	D	I
Birch Family:			
black birch	*Betula lenta*	P	
river birch	*Betula nigra*		I
paper birch	*Betula papyrifera*		I
gray birch	*Betula populifolia*		I

Appendix D. Woody plant species associated with vegetation alliances, predicted to occur, and/or inventoried during 2004 on the Schwoebel tract at Valley Forge National Historical Park (VAFO), Pennsylvania (continued).

Common Name[a]	Scientific Name	Doc./Pred.[b]	Inv.[c]
Birch Family (continued):			
hornbeam	*Carpinus caroliniana*	P	I
Linden Family:			
little-leaf linden	*Tilia cordata*		I
Willow Family:			
large-toothed aspen	*Populus grandidentata*		I
weeping willow	*Salix babylonica*		I
Heath Family:			
mountain laurel	*Kalmia latifolia*	D	
rosebay	*Rhododendron maximum*		I
blueberry	*Vaccinium* spp.	P	
Hydrangea Family:			
mock-orange	*Philadelphus* spp.		I
Rose Family:			
serviceberry	*Amelanchier* spp.		I
hawthorn	*Crataegus* spp.		I
crabapple	*Malus* spp.		I
Rose Family (continued):			
apple	*Malus pumila*	D	
sweet cherry or plum	*Prunus* spp.		I
wild black cherry	*Prunus serotina*	D	I
multiflora rose	*Rosa multiflora*	D	I
dewberry	*Rubus* spp.	D	I
wineberry	*Rubus phoenicolasius*	D	
Legume Family:			
false-indigo	*Amorpha fruticosa*		I
black locust	*Robinia pseudoacacia*	D	I
Chinese wisteria	*Wisteria sinensis*		I
Caesalpinia Family:			
Redbud	*Cercis canadensis*	D	
Honey-locust	*Gleditsia triacanthos*		I
Kentucky Coffee-tree	*Gymnocladus dioica*		I
Elaeagnus Family:			
autumn olive	*Elaeagnus umbellata*	D	I
Dogwood Family:			
black-gum	*Nyssa sylvatica*	D	I
kinnikinik	*Cornus amomum*		I
flowering dogwood	*Cornus florida*	D	I
swamp dogwood	*Cornus racemosa*		I
Bittersweet Family:			
oriental bittersweet	*Celastrus orbiculatus*	D	I
European spindle-tree	*Euonymus europaeus*		I

Appendix D. Woody plant species associated with vegetation alliances, predicted to occur, and/or inventoried during 2004 on the Schwoebel tract at Valley Forge National Historical Park (VAFO), Pennsylvania (continued).

Common Name[a]	Scientific Name	Doc./Pred.[b]	Inv.[c]
Holly Family:			
American holly	*Ilex opaca*		I
winterberry	*Ilex verticillata*		I
Grape Family:			
wild grape	*Vitis* spp.	D	I
summer grape	*Vitis aestivalis*	D	
Virginia creeper	*Parthenocissus quinquefolia*	P	I
Maple Family:			
box-elder	*Acer negundo*	D	I
Norway maple	*Acer platanoides*		I
red maple	*Acer rubrum*	D	I
silver maple	*Acer saccharinum*		I
sugar maple	*Acer saccharum*		I
Cashew Family:			
poison-ivy	*Toxicodendron radicans*	D	I
Quassia Family:			
tree-of-heaven	*Ailanthus altissima*	D	I
Olive Family:			
forsythia	*Forsythia* spp.		I
white ash	*Fraxinus americana*	D	I
common privet	*Ligustrum vulgare*	D	
common lilac	*Syringa vulgaris*		I
Trumpet-creeper Family:			
catalpa	*Catalpa* spp.		I
Honeysuckle Family:			
honeysuckle	*Lonicera* spp.	D	I
Japanese honeysuckle	*Lonicera japonica*	D	I
American elder	*Sambucus canadensis*		I
maple-leafed viburnum	*Viburnum acerifolium*	D	I
nannyberry	*Viburnum lentago*		I
black-haw	*Viburnum prunifolium*	D	
highbush-cranberry	*Viburnum trilobum*		I
linden arrow-wood	*Viburnum dilatatum*	D	I
Grass Family:			
bamboo	*Bambusa* spp.		I

[a]The vegetation-mapping project conducted at VAFO contained an alliance system for classifying vegetation; the predicted species list for Schwoebel tract was developed from species common to the four vegetation alliances (*Liriodendron tulipifera* Planted Forest, Successional Forest [Local Type], Successional Old Field/Shrubland [Local Type], and *Dactylis glomerata – Rumex acetosella* Cultivated Herbaceous) occurring on the tract (Lundgren et al. 2002).
[b]Documented or predicted: D = documented and commonly encountered in the four vegetation alliances at VAFO during the vegetation-mapping project (Lundgren et al. 2002); P = not commonly encountered in the four vegetation alliances at VAFO during the vegetation-mapping project, but common to the alliances on a global scale (Lundgren et al. 2002) and, therefore, predicted.
[c]Inventoried: I = recorded on the Schwoebel tract February–October, 2004.

Appendix E. Nomenclature and designation of cover-type classifications of vegetation communities occurring on the Schwoebel tract at Valley Forge National Historical Park (VAFO), Pennsylvania.

Alliance Description[a]	NVCS Alliance No.[b]	Cover Type[c]
Liriodendron tulipifera Planted Forest	I.B.2.N.a.24	Forest[d]
Successional Forest (Local Type)	-----	Successional
Successional Old Field / Shrubland (Local Type)	-----	Successional
Old Nursery Site	-----	Old Nursery
Dactylis glomerata - Rumex acetosella Cultivated Herbaceous	V.A.5.C.x.5	Grassland
Transportation Corridor	-----	Developed
Developed Land	-----	Developed

[a]Description of vegetation alliances presented in the vegetation-mapping project at VAFO (Lundgren et al. 2002).

[b]Alliance classification number, in accordance with the National Vegetation Classification System (NVCS) (Grossman et al. 1998; Lundgren et al. 2002). Alliance Numbers represented by ----- are not NVCS alliances.

[c]Cover type classification used to describe vegetation communities for the biotic inventory of the Schwoebel tract.

[d]Forest cover represents less than 1% total area of the Schwoebel tract.

Appendix F. Number of individuals for each herpetofauna species by sampling protocol and cover-type classification (Lundgren et al. 2002) detected from 9 February–28 October 2004 on the Schwoebel tract at Valley Forge National Historical Park, Pennsylvania.

Species	Common Name	Sampling Protocol[a]	Cover Type[b]				
			DEV	GRA	ONU	SUC	WAT
Salamanders	longtail salamander	ACO	0	0	2	0	0
		ACS	0	0	0	0	0
		GSS	0	0	0	0	9
		OOB	0	0	0	0	0
	northern dusky salamander	ACO	0	0	0	0	0
		ACS	0	0	0	0	0
		GSS	0	0	0	0	5
		OOB	0	0	0	0	0
	northern two-lined salamander	ACO	0	0	0	0	0
		ACS	0	0	0	0	0
		GSS	0	0	0	2	61
		OOB	0	0	0	0	0
	redback salamander	ACO	0	3	11	0	0
		ACS	0	0	0	0	0
		GSS	2	0	0	13	7
		OOB	0	0	0	0	0
Toads and frogs	eastern American toad	ACO	0	0	1	0	0
		ACS	0	0	0	0	0
		GSS	0	0	0	1	0
		OOB	3	0	1	0	0
	green frog	ACO	0	0	0	0	0
		ACS	0	0	0	0	0
		GSS	0	0	0	0	1
		OOB	0	0	5	0	0
	northern spring peeper	ACO	0	0	0	0	0
		ACS	0	0	0	8	0
		GSS	0	0	13	13	0
		OOB	0	0	6	0	0
	pickerel frog	ACO	0	0	0	0	0
		ACS	0	0	0	0	0
		GSS	0	0	6	1	15
		OOB	0	0	2	0	0
Turtles	eastern box turtle	ACO	0	0	0	0	0
		ACS	0	0	0	0	0
		GSS	0	0	0	1	0
		OOB	0	0	0	0	0
Snakes	eastern garter snake	ACO	0	0	6	0	0
		ACS	0	0	0	0	0
		GSS	0	0	0	0	0
		OOB	0	0	0	0	0
	northern black racer	ACO	0	3	1	0	0
		ACS	0	0	0	0	0
		GSS	0	0	0	0	0
		OOB	0	0	0	0	0

[a]Survey protocols include artificial cover-object transects (ACO), anuran-calling surveys (ACS), and general search surveys (GSS), and opportunistic observations (OOB).
[b]Cover type classifications include developed (DEV), grassland (GRA), old nursery (ONU), successional (SUC), and water (WAT).

Appendix G. Number of individuals for each mammal species by sampling protocol and cover-type classification (Lundgren et al. 2002) detected from 9 February–28 October 2004 on the Schwoebel tract at Valley Forge National Historical Park, Pennsylvania.

Species	Common name	Sampling protocol[a]	Cover type[b]			
			DEV	GRA	ONU	SUC
Opossums	Virginia opossum	LTR	0	0	1	0
		SLS	0	0	0	0
		OOB	2	0	0	0
Shrews	masked shrew	LTR	0	0	0	0
		SLS	0	0	0	0
		OOB	1	1	1	1
	northern short-tailed shrew	LTR	0	0	0	0
		SLS	0	0	0	0
		OOB	0	0	1	0
Rabbits	eastern cottontail	LTR	0	0	0	0
		SLS	0	0	0	0
		OOB	0	0	2	1
Squirrels	woodchuck	LTR	0	0	0	0
		SLS	0	0	0	0
		OOB	1	1	0	0
	eastern gray squirrel	LTR	0	0	0	0
		SLS	0	0	0	0
		OOB	2	0	4	0
New world mouse and vole	white-footed mouse	LTR	4	2	43	10
		SLS	0	0	0	0
		OOB	0	0	6	0
	meadow vole	LTR	0	1	6	0
		SLS	0	0	0	0
		OOB	0	4	1	0
Jumping mouse	meadow jumping mouse	LTR	0	0	0	0
		SLS	0	0	0	0
		OOB	0	0	1	0
Fox	red fox	LTR	0	0	0	0
		SLS	1	0	0	0
		OOB	8	0	1	0
Raccoon	common raccoon	LTR	0	0	0	1
		SLS	0	0	0	0
		OOB	1	0	1	0
Weasel	ermine or long-tailed weasel	LTR	0	0	0	0
		SLS	0	0	0	0
		OOB	1	0	0	0
Cat	domestic cat	LTR	0	0	0	0
		SLS	0	0	0	0
		OOB	1	0	0	0
Deer	white-tailed deer	LTR	0	0	0	0
		SLS	2	2	0	0
		OOB	0	0	1	0

[a]Survey Protocols include live-trapping (LTR), spotlighting surveys (SLS), and opportunistic observations (OOB).
[b]Cover type classifications include developed (DEV), grassland (GRA), old nursery (ONU), and successional (SUC).

Appendix H. Number of individuals for each bird species by cover-type classification (Lundgren et al. 2002) detected during the spring-migratory season (15 April–25 May) on the Schwoebel tract at Valley Forge National Historical Park, Pennsylvania. Number of individuals is presented for point-count surveys (PCS) followed by opportunistic observations (OOB) (i.e., PCS - OOB).

Species	Common name	Cover type[a]			
		DEV	GRA	ONU	SUC
Goose	Canada goose	0-0	1-0	0-0	2-0
New world vultures	turkey vulture	1-0	0-0	0-0	0-0
	black vulture	0-0	0-0	0-2	0-0
Dove	mourning dove	0-0	1-0	3-0	0-0
Cuckoo	black-billed cuckoo	0-0	1-0	3-0	0-0
Swift	chimney swift	3-0	0-0	2-3	1-0
Woodpeckers	northern flicker	0-0	2-0	1-0	0-0
	hairy woodpecker	0-0	0-0	0-0	0-1
Tyrant flycatcher	willow flycatcher	1-0	0-0	2-1	0-0
Vireos	white-eyed vireo	0-0	0-0	0-0	1-0
	red-eyed vireo	0-0	0-0	0-0	1-0
Jay and crow	blue jay	4-0	6-0	4-0	1-0
	American crow	2-0	0-0	2-0	1-0
Swallow	tree swallow	2-0	0-0	0-1	0-0
Titmouse and chickadee	tufted titmouse	0-0	0-0	3-0	0-0
	Carolina chickadee	2-0	2-0	5-0	2-0
Wrens	house wren	0-0	0-0	1-0	2-0
	Carolina wren	2-0	0-0	0-0	0-0
Kinglet	ruby-crowned kinglet	0-0	0-0	1-0	0-0
Gnatcatcher	blue-gray gnatcatcher	0-0	0-0	0-1	0-0
Thrushes	wood thrush	4-0	1-0	12-0	1-0
	American robin	5-0	6-0	6-0	2-0
Mockingbird	gray catbird	4-0	1-0	15-0	5-0
Starling	European starling	0-0	4-0	0-0	0-0
Waxwing	cedar waxwing	0-0	2-0	0-1	0-0
Wood-warblers	blue-winged warbler	0-0	1-0	3-0	1-0
	chestnut-sided warbler	0-0	0-0	0-3	0-0
	yellow-rumped warbler	0-0	0-0	3-0	0-0
	black-and-white warbler	0-0	0-0	1-0	0-0
	prairie warbler	0-0	0-0	0-1	0-0
	blackpoll warbler	0-0	0-0	1-0	1-1
	palm warbler	0-0	0-0	0-4	0-0
	yellow warbler	1-0	3-0	4-0	2-0
	Louisiana waterthrush	0-0	0-0	0-1	0-0
	northern waterthrush	0-0	0-0	0-1	0-0
	common yellowthroat	1-0	1-0	8-0	3-0
	American redstart	1-0	0-0	0-0	0-0
Emberizids	eastern towhee	1-0	0-0	0-0	0-0
	field sparrow	0-0	0-0	1-1	0-0
	song sparrow	1-0	7-0	5-0	0-0
	white-throated sparrow	2-0	1-0	1-0	3-0
	dark-eyed junco	0-0	0-0	1-0	0-0

Appendix H. Number of individuals for each bird species by cover-type classification (Lundgren et al. 2002) detected during the spring-migratory season (15 April–25 May) on the Schwoebel tract at Valley Forge National Historical Park, Pennsylvania. Number of individuals is presented for point-count surveys (PCS) followed by opportunistic observations (OOB) (i.e., PCS - OOB) (continued).

Species	Common name	Cover type[a]			
		DEV	GRA	ONU	SUC
Cardinals:	rose-breasted grosbeak	1-0	0-0	0-1	0-0
	northern cardinal	2-0	3-0	14-0	5-0
Blackbirds:	bobolink	0-0	0-1	0-0	0-0
	red-winged blackbird	0-0	8-0	6-0	0-0
	common grackle	0-0	1-0	0-0	0-0
	brown-headed cowbird	0-0	1-0	0-0	0-0
	Baltimore oriole	0-0	0-0	1-0	0-0
Finches:	house finch	0-0	2-0	0-0	0-0
	American goldfinch	1-0	3-0	5-0	0-0

[a]Cover type classifications include developed (DEV), grassland (GRA), old nursery (ONU), and successional (SUC).

Appendix I. Relative abundance (RA) (average number/point/survey) and standard deviation (SD) between sampling points of the most frequently detected long-distance migrant (LDM), short-distance migrant (SDM), and permanent-resident (PR) bird species identified using point-count surveys during the spring-migratory season (15 April–25 May 2004) on the Schwoebel tract at Valley Forge National Historical Park, Pennsylvania.

Species	Resident Status	RA + SD
gray catbird	SDM	1.79 + 1.19
northern cardinal	PR	1.71 + 1.14
American robin	PR	1.36 + 1.01
wood thrush	LDM	1.29 + 1.20
blue jay	PR	1.07 + 1.77
red-winged blackbird	SDM	1.00 + 2.15
song sparrow	PR	0.96 + 1.17
common yellowthroat	SDM	0.93 + 1.00
Carolina chickadee	PR	0.79 + 0.97
yellow warbler	LDM	0.71 + 0.91

Appendix J. Number of individuals for each bird species by cover-type classification (Lundgren et al. 2002) detected during the breeding season (25 May–15 July) using point-count surveys on the Schwoebel tract at Valley Forge National Historical Park, Pennsylvania.

Species	Common name	Cover Type[a]			
		DEV	GRA	ONU	SUC
Dove:	mourning dove	3	1	0	1
Swift:	chimney swift	4	1	8	0
Woodpeckers:	northern flicker	2	1	0	0
	downy woodpecker	0	1	0	0
Tyrant flycatcher:	willow flycatcher	0	1	0	0
Vireos:	white-eyed vireo	0	0	1	1
	red-eyed vireo	1	0	1	0
Jay and Crow:	blue jay	1	2	1	0
	American crow	1	0	0	0
Chickadee:	Carolina chickadee	0	0	2	0
Wren:	Carolina wren	1	0	1	0
Thrushes:	wood thrush	5	0	15	5
	American robin[b]	1	8	5	5
Mockingbird and Thrasher:	gray catbird	7	2	16	7
	brown thrasher	0	0	1	0
Starling:	European starling	2	6	0	0
Waxwing:	cedar waxwing	1	0	2	2
Wood-warblers:	yellow warbler	1	1	7	1
	common yellowthroat	3	2	13	3
Emberizids:	song sparrow	1	11	3	1
	white-throated sparrow	0	1	0	0
Cardinal:	northern cardinal	4	3	18	3
Blackbirds:	red-winged blackbird	0	8	1	0
	common grackle	0	2	0	0
	brown-headed cowbird	0	0	3	0
Finches:	house finch	0	3	0	0
	American goldfinch	0	1	4	0

[a]Cover type classifications include developed (DEV), grassland (GRA), old nursery (ONU), and successional (SUC).
[b]An opportunistic observation was made of American robin in developed cover type.

Appendix K. Relative abundance (RA) (average number/point/survey) and standard deviation (SD) between sampling points of the most frequently detected long-distance migrant (LDM), short-distance migrant (SDM), and permanent-resident (PR) bird species identified using point-count surveys during the breeding season (25 May–15 July 2004) on the Schwoebel tract at Valley Forge National Historical Park, Pennsylvania.

Species	Resident Status	RA + SD
gray catbird	SDM	2.29 + 1.07
northern cardinal	PR	2.00 + 1.30
wood thrush	LDM	1.79 + 1.42
common yellowthroat	SDM	1.50 + 0.65
American robin	PR	1.36 + 1.50
song sparrow	PR	1.14 + 1.96
chimney swift	LDM	0.93 + 2.06
yellow warbler	LDM	0.71 + 0.73
red-winged blackbird	SDM	0.64 + 1.65
European starling	PR	0.57 + 1.16

Appendix L. Number of individuals for each bird species by cover-type classification (Lundgren et al. 2002) detected during the fall-migratory season (25 August–10 October) on the Schwoebel tract at Valley Forge National Historical Park, Pennsylvania. Number of individuals is presented for point-count surveys (PCS) followed by opportunistic observations (OOB) (i.e., PCS - OOB).

Species	Common name	Cover Type[a]			
		DEV	GRA	ONU	SUC
Goose:	Canada goose	0-0	4-0	3-0	0-0
Dove:	mourning dove	0-0	3-0	0-0	1-0
Woodpeckers:	northern flicker	1-0	0-0	1-0	0-0
	downy woodpecker	2-0	0-0	2-1	1-0
Tyrant Flycatcher:	eastern phoebe	0-0	0-0	0-0	1-0
Vireo:	blue-headed vireo	2-0	0-0	0-1	0-0
Jays and Crow:	blue jay	3-0	3-0	3-0	0-0
	American crow	10-0	0-0	3-0	0-0
Titmouse and Chickadee:	tufted titmouse	2-0	3-0	4-0	2-0
	Carolina chickadee	3-0	0-0	12-0	0-0
Nuthatch:	white-breasted nuthatch	1-0	0-0	0-0	1-0
Wren:	Carolina wren	1-0	0-0	2-0	1-0
Kinglet:	ruby-crowned kinglet	1-0	0-0	0-0	0-0
Thrushes:	eastern bluebird	0-0	2-0	2-0	1-0
	veery	0-0	0-0	1-0	0-0
	American robin	12-75	12-0	74-0	13-0
Mockingbird and Thrasher:	gray catbird	3-0	3-0	11-0	3-0
	northern mockingbird	0-0	2-0	0-0	0-0
Starling:	Eeuropean starling	0-0	4-0	0-0	0-0
Waxwing:	cedar waxwing	0-0	0-0	7-0	2-0
Wood-warblers:	Nashville warbler	0-0	0-0	0-1	0-0
	magnolia warbler	0-0	0-0	0-2	0-0
	yellow-rumped warbler	0-0	4-0	0-30	0-0
	black-throated green warbler	2-0	0-0	0-3	0-0
	American redstart	1-0	0-0	0-0	0-0
Emberizids:	eastern towhee	0-0	0-0	1-0	0-0
	song sparrow	0-0	1-0	1-0	0-0
	white-throated sparrow	1-0	0-0	0-0	2-0
Cardinal:	northern cardinal	2-0	2-0	4-0	3-0
Blackbird:	brown-headed cowbird	0-0	6-0	0-0	0-0
Finches:	house finch	2-0	8-0	4-0	2-0
	American goldfinch	1-0	2-0	2-0	1-0

[a]Cover type classifications include developed (DEV), grassland (GRA), old nursery (ONU), and successional (SUC).

65

Appendix M. Relative abundance (RA) (average number/point/survey) and standard deviation (SD) between sampling points of the most frequently detected short-distance migrant (SDM) and permanent-resident (PR) bird species identified using point-count surveys during the fall-migratory season (25 August–10 October 2004) on the Schwoebel tract at Valley Forge National Historical Park, Pennsylvania.

Species	Resident Status	RA + SD
American robin	PR	7.86 + 9.17
gray catbird	SDM	1.43 + 0.85
house finch	PR	1.14 + 1.92
Carolina chickadee	PR	1.07 + 1.38
American crow	PR	0.93 + 2.46
tufted titmouse	PR	0.79 + 1.05
northern cardinal	PR	0.79 + 0.80
blue jay	PR	0.64 + 0.74
cedar waxwing	PR	0.64 + 1.39
Canada goose	PR	0.50 + 1.16

Appendix N. Number of individuals for each bird species by cover-type classification (Lundgren et al. 2002) detected during the winter season (1 December–30 March) on the Schwoebel tract at Valley Forge National Historical Park, Pennsylvania. Number of individuals is presented for point-count surveys (PCS) followed by opportunistic observations (OOB) (i.e., PCS - OOB). No avian species were detected while conducting the owl survey protocol.

Species	Cover Type[a]			
	DEV	GRA	ONU	SUC
Goose:				
Canada goose	0-0	11-0	30-0	0-0
New World Vulture:				
turkey vulture	0-0	0-0	5-0	0-0
Hawks:				
Cooper's hawk	0-0	2-0	1-0	0-0
red-shouldered hawk	0-0	0-0	1-0	0-0
red-tailed hawk	2-0	1-0	0-1	1-0
Sandpiper:				
American woodcock	0-0	0-0	0-7	0-0
Gull:				
herring gull	1-0	0-0	0-0	0-0
Doves:				
rock dove	1-0	4-0	3-0	0-0
mourning dove	0-0	2-0	0-2	1-0
Owl:				
great horned owl	0-0	0-0	0-1	0-0
Woodpeckers:				
red-bellied woodpecker	0-0	0-0	0-0	2-0
northern flicker	0-0	0-0	1-0	0-0
downy woodpecker	0-0	0-0	1-1	0-0
hairy woodpecker	0-0	1-0	0-0	0-0
Tyrant Flycatcher:				
eastern phoebe	0-2	0-0	0-0	0-0
Jay and Crow:				
blue jay	0-0	1-0	6-0	0-0
American crow	1-0	0-0	5-0	1-0
Titmouse and Chickadee:				
tufted titmouse	1-0	3-0	8-0	3-0
Carolina chickadee	4-0	5-0	12-0	2-0
Nuthatch:				
white-breasted nuthatch	0-0	0-0	1-0	1-0
Wren:				
Carolina wren	0-0	1-0	1-0	0-1
Kinglets:				
golden-crowned kinglet	0-0	0-0	2-2	0-0
ruby-crowned kinglet	0-0	0-0	1-0	0-0
Thrush:				
American robin	0-0	15-0	1-59	1-0
Mockingbird:				
northern mockingbird	0-0	1-0	1-1	0-0

Appendix N. Number of individuals for each bird species by cover-type classification (Lundgren et al. 2002) detected during the winter season (1 December–30 March) on the Schwoebel tract at Valley Forge National Historical Park, Pennsylvania. Number of individuals is presented for point-count surveys (PCS) followed by opportunistic observations (OOB) (i.e., PCS - OOB). No avian species were detected while conducting the owl survey protocol (continued).

Species	Cover Type[a]			
	DEV	GRA	ONU	SUC
Starling:				
European starling	0-0	0-0	1-0	0-0
Wood-warbler:				
yellow-rumped warbler	0-0	1-0	1-0	0-0
Emberizids:				
American tree sparrow	0-0	0-3	0-0	0-0
song sparrow	0-0	1-0	0-1	0-0
white-throated sparrow	0-0	4-0	3-0	0-0
dark-eyed junco	0-0	0-0	2-1	0-0
Cardinal:				
Northern cardinal	4-0	0-0	8-0	1-0
Blackbirds:				
red-winged blackbird	0-0	35-0	0-0	0-4
common grackle	0-0	0-0	0-3	0-0
Finches:				
purple finch	0-0	0-0	1-0	0-0
house finch	0-0	1-0	6-0	2-0
American goldfinch	0-0	1-0	3-0	0-0

[a]Cover type classifications include developed (DEV), grassland (GRA), old nursery (ONU), and successional (SUC).

Appendix O. Relative abundance (RA) (average number/point/survey) and standard deviation (SD) between sampling points of the most frequently detected short-distance migrant (SDM) and permanent-resident (PR) bird species identified using point-count surveys during the winter season (1 December, 2003–15 March 2004) on the Schwoebel tract at Valley Forge National Historical Park, Pennsylvania.

Species	Resident Status	RA + SD
Canada goose	PR	2.93 + 8.32
red-winged blackbird	SDM	2.50 + 9.35
Carolina chickadee	PR	1.64 + 1.28
American robin	PR	1.21 + 3.02
tufted titmouse	PR	1.07 + 0.92
northern cardinal	PR	0.93 + 1.07
house finch	PR	0.64 + 1.60
rock dove	PR	0.57 + 1.28
blue jay	PR	0.50 + 0.76
American crow	PR	0.50 + 0.85
white-throated sparrow	SDM	0.50 + 0.85

NPS D-089 November 2006